RESTORING ORDER AND GIVING HOPE

THE OKLAHOMA NATIONAL GUARD RESPONSE TO HURRICANE KATRINA

BY **BOB BURKE** AND COLONEL **MAX MOSS,** JR. (RET.)

Gini Moore Campbell, Series Editor
Natalie Taylor, Assistant Series Editor

OKLAHOMA HALL *of* FAME
—————————————————
OKLAHOMA HERITAGE ASSOCIATION PUBLISHING

OKLAHOMA HALL *of* FAME

The authors are grateful to the dozens of Soldiers and Airmen, many who had left military service, who were willing to be interviewed for this book and share their unique Hurricane Katrina stories. It is through their distinctive personal experience we can see the tremendous courage and resilience of the great people of Louisiana and Mississippi and how Oklahoma National Guardsmen made their life tolerable in a time of great emergency.

CONTENTS

PREFACE

Hurricane Katrina was the most destructive natural disaster in the history of the United States. In late August and early September, 2005, the storm devastated 90,000 square miles of American soil with 140-mile-per-hour winds and torrential rain. The aftermath was catastrophic for several states along the Gulf Coast, leaving nearly 2,000 people dead and more than $100 billion in damage.

The greatest toll in human suffering and loss of property came in New Orleans. Levee breaches led to massive flooding and mass evacuations. Lack of adequate planning and preparation by federal, state, and local governments exacerbated the plight of people who had no means, or flatly refused, to evacuate. Some people were trapped in attics and nursing homes and drowned as the dirty waters engulfed them. Others escaped by chopping their way through roofs and waiting for rescue.

The storm laid waste to much of the New Orleans police force, whose headquarters and several district offices, along with hundreds of vehicles and ammunition depots, were destroyed by raging waters. Even with the help of local National Guard troops, chaos gripped the city.

The famous Superdome, site of Super Bowls and college championships, became the "shelter of last resort" for 30,000 storm victims. Mayhem ensued, with rape, murder, and suicide reported. The people were hungry, angry, and afraid. When the storm ripped two large sections from the Superdome roof, water poured into the once proud arena and unbelievable conditions persisted.

As the national tragedy unfolded, the call for help was sounded from the White House and Louisiana Governor's Mansion. The response of the Oklahoma National

Guard was timely and of great magnitude. Within a few minutes of being activated, units quickly activated an emergency plan to move personnel and equipment to New Orleans. Once on the ground, it made no difference whether they were infantry or artillerymen, headquarters units, or air guardsmen, all Oklahoma troops rolled up their sleeves and went to work saving lives and property.

Men and women of the Oklahoma National Guard left behind families, jobs, and school to carry out their assignments in the most trying of conditions. Sections of the city were patrolled in eight-man squads. Every patrol was a dirty, dangerous, and gruesome job that Oklahoma soldiers performed with the same seriousness they used to approach combat when deployed to Afghanistan or Iraq. Guardsmen will never forget wading through a gagging brown slush of flood water that was a hybrid of decaying bodies and ruptured sewer pipes.

When it was over, Louisiana Governor Kathleen Blanco thanked the Oklahoma Guardsmen for "saving the day" for her people. The praise was deserved. Oklahoma units were in the thick of it in New Orleans, helping rescue storm survivors, restore order from the chaos, and locate bodies of the more than 1,500 killed in the city.

The Oklahoma National Guard response was no surprise. The Guard has always responded quickly and efficiently, both in natural disaster or disorder at home and in military operations overseas.

This book is the story of more than 2,000 men and women of the Oklahoma National Guard—and their heroic efforts during the days following the destruction of one of America's largest and most-celebrated cities.

Members of Company B, 700th Support Battalion pose for a group photo near a United States Navy cargo ship.

FOREWORD

Albert Ashwood
Director, Oklahoma Department of Emergency Management

Oklahomans know and have come to expect that when serious disaster strikes our State, the National Guard will be there right alongside civilian first responders to provide assistance as needed. The confidence we place in the Guard and in the men and women in uniform is well deserved because they have never let our State down.

In 2005, Hurricane Katrina struck the gulf coast and the National Guard once again stepped up to assist. While much was written about Hurricane Katrina during and immediately after the storm, lost in the shuffle was the Oklahoma National Guard's story at New Orleans. Renowned Oklahoma author Bob Burke and Col. (Ret.) Max Moss have gone back in time to collect the firsthand accounts of the Oklahoma Citizen Soldiers and Airmen who responded at a moment's notice to help those devastated by the storm.

The major news networks that covered the destruction caused by Hurricane Katrina had dozens of stories to tell every day—stories about the tremendously resilient and brave people who called New Orleans home, and those who came from around the world to help them. However, all too often, these positive, uplifting stories were overshadowed by reports of crime and corruption.

More than a decade later, Burke and Moss have diligently interviewed dozens about their Katrina experience. Their book brings to life a story that long ago needed to be told, not because these brave men and women seek recognition, but for the reason that what they did for the people of New Orleans may be the greatest Guard story that *no one* has ever heard.

I've been privileged to work alongside the Oklahoma National Guard for many years after acts of domestic terrorism, devastating tornadoes, and torrential flooding. Their remarkable capacity to respond in support of first responders is a vital component in our ability as a state to come to the aide of our citizens.

RESTORING ORDER
AND GIVING HOPE

CHAPTER ONE

CHAOS AND ANARCHY

New Orleans descended into anarchy as corpses lay abandoned on streets, fights and fires broke out, and the tired and hungry seethed, saying they had been forsaken.

An Associated Press dispatch on September 1, 2005

La Nouvelle-Orleans (New Orleans) was founded along the Mississippi River on May 7, 1718, by French colonists. Named for the French Duke of Orleans, Phillipe II, the city is known as the Big Easy, the Crescent City, and NOLA. After Napoleon Bonaparte sold Louisiana to the United States in the Louisiana Purchase in 1803, New Orleans grew rapidly with a blend of Americans, French, Creoles, and Africans.

In two centuries of flying the American flag, New Orleans became one of the most unique and recognizable cities in the world. Known for its distinct French and Spanish Creole architecture, as well as its cross-cultural and multilingual heritage and cuisine, New Orleans was the birthplace of jazz. People from all over the world flocked to the city for its annual celebrations and festivals, most notably *Mardi Gras,* dating to French colonial times.

With all its charm, New Orleans was always at risk in the event the city took a direct hit from a major hurricane. Although about half the city actually lies above sea level, its average elevation is about six feet below sea level, and it is completely surrounded by water.

During the 20th century, the United States Army Corps of Engineers constructed a system of seawalls and levees to keep the city from flooding. Along the Mississippi River, the levees were trustworthy, but the ones built to hold back Lake Pontchartrain and the waterlogged marshes and swamps on the east and west sides of the city were less reliable. For decades, officials had warned that storm surge could overtop some levees and cause short-term flooding.

In 2001, the Federal Emergency Management Agency (FEMA) identified the three most likely disasters to strike the nation: an earthquake in California, a terrorist attack in New York City, and a hurricane in New Orleans. But no one predicted that levees might collapse and put in danger neighborhoods that lay below sea level, neighborhoods in which the city's poorest and most vulnerable people lived. Then, the unimaginable happened in August, 2005.

A satellite view of Hurricane Katrina as it approaches the Gulf Coast. *Courtesy National Weather Service.*

It began on August 24 as a tropical depression southeast of Florida, but soon the storm was upgraded to hurricane status and named Katrina. Four people were killed in Florida and more than a million customers were without electricity. Regenerating over the Gulf of Mexico, Katrina turned northward and the governors of Mississippi

and Louisiana declared a state of emergency.

The National Hurricane Center cited a computer model of a powerful storm over-topping levees protecting New Orleans and surrounding parishes. One weatherman said, "This is scary, this is the real thing." The head of the National Hurricane Center told New Orleans Mayor Ray Nagin, "I've never seen a hurricane like this in my 33-year career. You need to order mandatory evacuation. Get as many people out as possible."

On Sunday, August 28, Mayor Nagin issued a mandatory evacuation. In a city in which more than 100,000 people did not own cars, city buses ran constantly, taking residents of threatened areas to the Louisiana Superdome, a cavernous sports venue in downtown New Orleans. Mayor Nagin called the Superdome "the shelter of last resort." The Louisiana National Guard was activated and the United States Coast Guard mobilized to respond after the storm hit.

At daybreak on Monday, August 29, Hurricane Katrina came ashore with 140-mile-per-hour sustained winds. The storm's eye passed east of New Orleans, but accompanying winds ripped a hole in the Superdome, knocking out power. High water from torrential rain began flowing over the levees. The city police department was overwhelmed when floodwaters overran its headquarters and several district command posts. The Louisiana National Guard's Jackson Barracks flooded and some guardsmen spent the next 24 hours just trying to stay alive and salvage equipment needed in other parts of the city.

Beleaguered city and state officials received

A Louisiana National Guardsman surveys the massive flooding in low-lying areas of New Orleans. *Courtesy FEMA.*

With few local National Guardsmen, police, and firemen to help, residents of flooded areas were left to fend for themselves. *Courtesy* New Orleans Times-Picayune.

reports of breaks in the Industrial Canal and 17th Street Canal levees. Flooding grew as water surged over breaches in the levees from Lake Ponchartrain. Water seeped through the soil underneath some levees and swept others away altogether. The 9th Ward was almost entirely submerged, the 911 system was clogged, and looting broke out in parts of the city.

The city's water supply was instantly polluted. The storm's surge flooded three Superfund toxic waste sites in the New Orleans area and destroyed or contaminated more than 150 drinking water facilities and 47 wastewater treatment plants along the Gulf Coast. Emergency responders were exposed to water filled with chemicals, decomposing bodies, bacteria, oil and gas, and dangerous debris.

On Tuesday, August 30, hotels turned out guests who, along with thousands of residents, broke into the Morial Convention Center, looking for anyplace to lay down and rest. Officials hoped the nearby Superdome could house 15,000 people, but its population exploded to 30,000. Conditions deteriorated, there was no power for air conditioning, and little food and water. There were reports of rape and at least one murder. Another man committed suicide by jumping from an upper level. Outside, thousands more rushed toward a helicopter trying to drop food. The chopper could not land and was forced to drop supplies into the crowd and fly away.

When Louisiana Governor Kathleen Blanco toured the Superdome, she announced it should be evacuated because of still-rising water and

When levees failed, entire neighborhoods were flooded.

A mother clings to her children, looking for safe haven in the aftermath of Katrina. *Courtesy* New Orleans Times-Picayune.

uninhabitable conditions. Rescue efforts were delayed because virtually all communications systems were knocked out. Eighty percent of New Orleans was under water. FEMA chartered nearly 500 buses to move people from the Superdome, but they were painfully slow in coming. Patients and staff were stranded at hospitals with emergency power dwindling. Widespread looting continued. Shots rang out as store owners tried to defend their property from looters. New Orleans had descended into anarchy.

An Associated Press reporter saw seven bodies scattered outside the convention center, a makeshift staging area for residents rescued from rooftops. People roamed sidewalks with no food, water, or medical care. There was no sign of law enforcement. The street outside the convention center smelled of urine and feces. Dirty diapers, old bottles, and other garbage was stacked everywhere, sometimes choking the sidewalk as a passageway.

The crowd chanted, "We want help. We want help." Occasionally, a state police car filled with officers in riot gear passed, but there was no other sign of help. After the tragedy, FEMA Director Michael Brown admitted he should have called in the military earlier because all units of government, from the federal to the parish level, were totally overwhelmed and unequipped to deal with the magnitude of the destruction of Hurricane Katrina.

A horrible stench began to emanate from the Big Easy. Decaying bodies and ruptured sewage lines made it nearly unbearable for the

Death was everywhere. An old man's body was
abandoned on a chaise lounge in a street median.
An elderly woman lay dead in her wheelchair.
Someone had respectfully laid a tattered blanket
over her. The people were frustrated and without hope.

Relief agencies such as the Salvation Army were totally overwhelmed
with the massive number of people in need in New Orleans.
Courtesy New Orleans Times-Picayune.

A desperate woman begs for help outside the Louisiana Superdome.
Courtesy Oklahoma Publishing Company.

Hurricane Katrina removed a portion of the roof of the Superdome, cutting off power, and allowing water to pour into the overcrowded facility.

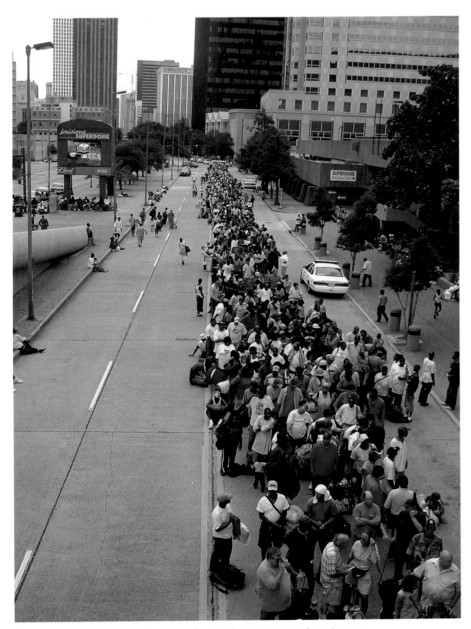

HURRICANE KATRINA FACTS

- The total damage was estimated at $108 billion.

- More than one million people in the Gulf region were displaced, more than in the Dust Bowl that plagued the Southern Plains during the Great Depression.

- Private insurance companies paid an estimated $41 billion on nearly two million claims.

- 1,833 people were killed, 1,577 of them in Louisiana. Nearly half the fatalities were people over the age of 74. 40% of the deaths were by drowning.

- Seventy percent of New Orleans' occupied housing, 134,000 units, was damaged.

- The population of New Orleans decreased more than 50% from 2005 to 2006.

Hurricane survivors were lined up for blocks to try to gain entrance into the Superdome. *Courtesy* New Orleans Times-Picayune.

A handful of police and guardsmen try to placate thousands waiting for buses outside the Superdome.

A child is comforted by adults that surrounded her, waiting in a line for food and water. *Courtesy* New Orleans Times-Picayune.

living. Death was everywhere. An old man's body was abandoned on a chaise lounge in a street median. An elderly woman lay dead in her wheelchair. Someone had respectfully laid a tattered blanket over her. The people were frustrated and without hope.

Mayor Nagin ordered the police force to abandon search and rescue missions and turn its attention toward control of looting and gunfights. A local newspaper reported that when a tourist asked a police officer for help, the officer said, "Go to hell, it's every man for himself." Nagin called for increased federal assistance in a "desperate S.O.S." Limited relief efforts were disrupted by violence and there were reports of groups of armed men running through the streets, pillaging unattended buildings and stores. Charity Hospital, one of several hospitals desperately trying to evacuate patients, had to halt efforts after coming under gunfire.

Meanwhile, bad turned to worse at the Superdome. "We pee on the floor. We are like animals," a young mother said as she cradled her three-week-old son. Baby supplies were rare. One mother said she was given two diapers and told to scrape them off when they got dirty and use them again.

Five hundred Louisiana National Guardsmen were understandably overwhelmed by the chaos. Many carried machine guns as the human masses pressed against metal barricades that kept them from leaving, shouting to the soldiers, "Hey! We need more water! We need help!"

Promised buses from FEMA did not arrive or were delayed. There were reports of rampant

Most of the houses that stood after the fierce winds of Hurricane Katrina were not inhabitable. *Courtesy Oklahoma Publishing Company.*

President George W. Bush toured the stricken area and recognized the inadequacy of the federal response. He heartily endorsed the arrival of National Guardsmen to restore order and lend assistance to victims. *Courtesy New Orleans Fire Department.*

Thousands of automobiles and homes were inundated by flood waters. *Courtesy New Orleans Fire Department.*

A frightened dog swims for safety as flood waters rise in the Ninth Ward of New Orleans. *Courtesy* New Orleans Times-Picayune.

drug use, fights, and filthy living conditions. Governor Blanco declared a public health emergency and ordered a mandatory evacuation for all residents in flooded areas.

"It's like downtown Baghdad," a tourist reflected as she saw dead bodies and trash littering the street. Emergency responders used every means available to help. Doctors in their scrubs used canoes to take supplies to blacked-out hospitals. "It was like being in a Third World country," said a nurse at Charity Hospital, where nurses were ventilating patients by hand. Rescue teams were plucking people from rooftops and leaving them on highway overpasses to wait to be moved again.

New Orleans was sinking deeper into crisis. United States Senator Mary Landrieu flew over the 9th Ward and saw a group of people smash a window at a convenience store. At a drug store in the French Quarter, people ran out with grocery baskets and coolers full of soft drinks, diapers, and chips. One looter shot and wounded a fellow looter. Only rooftops were visible in many neighborhoods. Many homes

were on fire, sparked by ruptured gas lines.

By any measure, Hurricane Katrina was a national catastrophe. The images of suffering despair from victims tugged at the hearts of all Americans who watched in horror as reporters attempted to describe the plight of one of America's great cities. Against the backdrop of human suffering and never-before-seen destruction of property, an ill-prepared government cried out to the American military. After a jurisdictional fight among leaders, it was decided that the military provided the only solution to the unfolding nightmare. The call for help went out from the White House and Louisiana to neighboring states. In the next 40 days, the Oklahoma National Guard would come to the rescue and play a prominent role in the incredible response of the American military.

In addition to the human tragedy, tens of thousands of pets were stranded by flood waters. *Courtesy* New Orleans Times-Picayune.

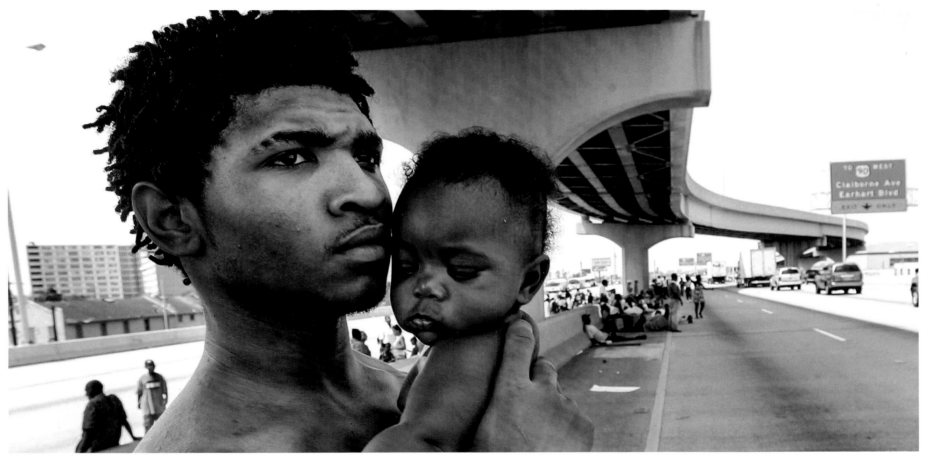

A father holds his baby while huddled under a bridge trying to escape the hot sun. *Courtesy Oklahoma Publishing Company.*

Members of the Army National Guard's Quick Reaction Force get some sleep while flying to New Orleans on September 1, 2005.

CHAPTER TWO

TASK FORCE OKLAHOMA

We were called and we answered the call. It was truly a team effort. Army Guard and Air Guard coming together to get our troops to the fight "on time, on target."

Major General Harry M. "Bud" Wyatt, III
Adjutant General for Oklahoma

The Oklahoma National Guard always has been ready for any emergency when activated for war service or peacetime natural disaster. One of the first acts of the Oklahoma Territorial Legislature in 1890 was to create a State Militia, renamed the National Guard in 1895. At statehood in 1907, National Guard units were established in the former Oklahoma and Indian territories. Before World War I, Governor Lee Cruce used the National Guard to combat illegal boxing and horse racing operations.

Oklahoma guardsmen were mobilized in 1917 in World War I for service in France. Between the world wars, the National Guard was frequently used by governors for various duties, from preventing the legislature from convening to shutting down oil production in the Seminole Oil Field. In World War II, the 45th Infantry Division was federally activated with troops serving in the Panama Canal Zone, the Southwest Pacific, Alaska, and Okinawa. But the bulk of the 45th soldiers were sent to Sicily in 1943 and fought in some of the war's bloodiest campaigns in Italy,

France, and Central Europe. The Thunderbirds of the Oklahoma 45th Division became part of the legend of the American military.

In modern times, Oklahoma Army National Guard units were activated by governors to help fellow citizens deal with floods, fires, tornadoes, or other emergency situations, to quiet trouble at state prisons, and to drop hay to stranded livestock after blizzards struck the state. Guard units helped state law enforcement officials eradicate millions of marijuana plants and helped with other drug enforcement missions. After the Oklahoma City bombing of the Alfred P. Murrah Federal Building in 1995, National Guard personnel provided security, rescue, and recovery help.

In the new century, guardsmen were activated by the President for the war in Afghanistan and Iraq. When the call for help came for Katrina, some guardsmen had been home only a few months from a Middle East deployment.

Even before Katrina became a major disaster, Oklahoma National Guard leaders were making plans. Adjutant General, Major General Harry M. "Bud" Wyatt, III, of Ketchum, came home early from a family trip to the lake to plan for the probability that Oklahoma Guard units would be deployed. Oklahoma had 10,000 National Guardsmen—7,500 in the Army National Guard and 2,500 in the Air National Guard. However, several units were still deployed in Afghanistan and Iraq. For several years, Oklahoma units had rotated in the desert with personnel and equipment to supplement the war effort.

Even with operating at less than full force,

Oklahoma was in a unique position. Unlike other states with National Guard structure connected to several states, Oklahoma was self-contained and could exercise command and control over a vast majority of its units. Early in the planning, General Wyatt talked by telephone with Oklahoma Governor Brad Henry. The governor was completely supportive of Oklahoma Guardsmen helping neighbors in need, but was concerned that the state might not have sufficient funds on hand to pay what General Wyatt estimated could cost one million dollars a day.

Even when Governor Henry could not be guaranteed that the federal government would bear the cost, he gave General Wyatt the authority to commit Oklahoma troops. The governor said, "People need help. We will respond to the extent we can and worry about the money later." General Wyatt requested authority to send up to 2,500 guardsmen to the Gulf Coast.

The day before Katrina made landfall, Oklahoma National Guard officials were in communication with the Pentagon about the potential activation of state units to assist in the predicted disaster in New Orleans. Major John Zenker, of Plano, Texas, an Oklahoma National Guardsman temporarily assigned to the Army Operations Center at the Pentagon, briefed the Secretary of the Army and Army senior staff daily in regard to the funding and manpower needed to move military forces, including National Guard troops, into the region struck by Katrina.

Zenker watched Katrina's path and alerted

The governor said, "People need help. We will respond to the extent we can and worry about the money later."

Major General Harry M. Wyatt, III, the Adjutant General for Oklahoma, talks to reporters after Governor Brad Henry, left, announced plans to send Oklahoma guardsmen to Louisiana and the Gulf Coast.

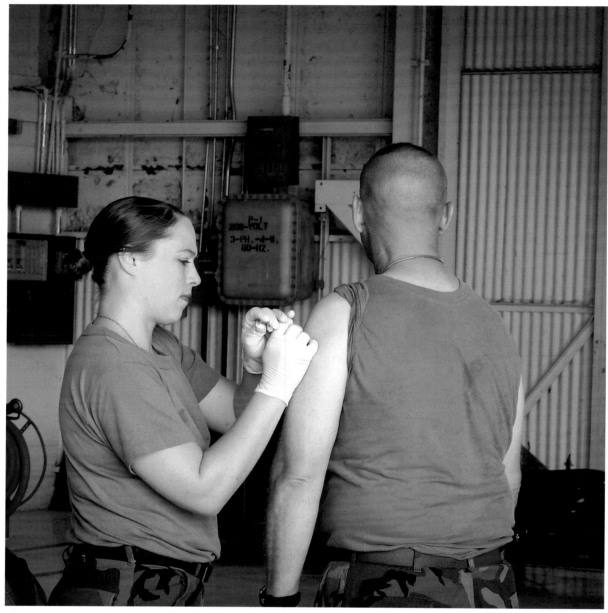

All Oklahoma National Guardsmen received shots before traveling to the Gulf Coast.

senior Army staff of the potential for a major disaster. "It was pretty chaotic," Zenker remembered. "We were fighting a war in the Middle East, but top brass wanted to be ready to commit troops, money, and equipment to support victims of Katrina." When the storm hit, Zenker had eyes on the ground in New Orleans in the form of his brother-in-law, a surgeon at a New Orleans hospital. During a scratchy cell-phone conversation, Zenker learned of chaos and suffering in the city, the hospital pharmacy being ransacked, and gunfire heard outside the emergency room door. Zenker passed along the first hand information to his superiors.

General Wyatt was constantly in touch with his counterpart in Louisiana. When Wyatt said he could commit up to 2,500 troops, Louisiana authorities were overwhelmed with the offer to help. General Wyatt said, "Well, just put that offer in your hip pocket and we will see what happens and if you need that many boots on the ground."

General Wyatt ordered the Joint Force Headquarters to begin operation in the basement of the Oklahoma Military Department headquarters. It was made up of officers and senior NCO's (non-commissioned officers) from both the Army and Air National Guard. Its purpose was to begin planning for deployment of men and equipment. Lieutenant Colonel Jim Pahdoco of Oklahoma City was the Oklahoma National Guard's director of military support to civil authorities and began assessing resources. Pahdoco said, "We had to plan big, committing 2,000 troops right away. But, you couldn't put people in until it was clear."

Major Anthony Georgiades, left, and Captain Hiram Tabler at work in the Joint Operations Center.

Brigadier General Myles L. Deering was chosen to head Task Force Oklahoma.

As a second levee broke in New Orleans, flooding 80 percent of the city, Louisiana Governor Kathleen Blanco called Oklahoma Governor Henry and governors of surrounding states to plead for immediate assistance. The plea for help came as a result of the Emergency Management Assistance Compact (EMAC), a national mutual aid and partnership agreement that allows state-to-state assistance during a state of emergency. General Wyatt later said, "The use of EMAC during Hurricane Katrina, by providing a responsive system for the use of National Guard troops in states unaffected by a disaster, is a testament to effective use of resources when local National Guard units are overwhelmed."

President George W. Bush declared a federal disaster, so Oklahoma National Guardsmen closely watched news accounts of the chaos in New Orleans, expecting to be called to active duty at any time. Medical officers at armories around the state began checking soldiers' records to make certain they were current for Hepatitis A and B and Tetanus shots required for a deployment to Louisiana.

General Wyatt selected Brigadier General Myles L. Deering of Norman, commander of the 45th Infantry Brigade, to head the operation called Task Force Oklahoma. Governor Henry issued an Executive Order that recognized Hurricane Katrina as "an emergency of national magnitude" and that it was necessary to declare a disaster emergency in Oklahoma so that the National Guard, the Department of Emergency Management, and other state and local governments could "adequately respond" to the mutual aid requests from Louisiana, Mississippi, Alabama, and Florida. The governor's chief of staff, Gerald Adams, emailed Adjutant General Wyatt, "The Governor has just told me directly that he approves your participation and to go full steam ahead."

The original grant of authority to General Wyatt was up to 2,500 Guardsmen in support of Katrina relief. But when the National Guard Bureau estimated that more troops might be needed, the general asked the governor to expand the authority to 2,900. Wyatt wrote, "I am drawing the line at 3,000 guardsmen as we need sufficient stay-behind force to handle any potential Oklahoma state emergency missions." Within 45 minutes of the request, Chief of Staff Adams responded, "You have the Governor's approval. We will do paperwork later."

Sergeant Major David Keating of Noble, the state Command Sergeant, said morale was high among Oklahoma National Guardsmen who were watching the news and anticipating being activated. Keating said, "This is citizens helping citizens. Oklahoma soldiers are always ready to help their neighbors. They have no qualms about jumping into the situation."

As personnel availability was assessed by unit personnel around the state, the follow-on force 45th Infantry Brigade sent a directive that guardsmen who were enrolled in college should be left off the activation list. However, to be part of the mission, many guardsmen notified instructors they were on standby to go to New Orleans.

Joint Operations Center staff briefing.

National Guard vehicles lined up outside the 23rd Street Armory in Oklahoma City, waiting for troops to head to New Orleans.

The Oklahoma National Guard was incredibly prepared for planning a unique mission to Louisiana. Just three years prior to Katrina, a full brigade convoy was launched to Alexandria, Louisiana, for training. For 45th Infantry Battalion Personnel Officer Major Scott Houck of Norman, the 2002 operation prepared his staff for the laborious task of preparing manifests for moving people and equipment from dozens of Oklahoma armories to another state. In addition, Houck said the Oklahoma Guard's experience in Afghanistan and Iraq prepared its soldiers for daily-changing missions in extreme circumstances.

Oklahoma's involvement in New Orleans began with a request for two UH-60 Black Hawk helicopters equipped with rescue hoists. There were reports of thousands of people stranded, with many residents seeking shelter on rooftops and in trees.

The nine guardsmen who made up the crews of the Black Hawks were the first Oklahoma National Guardsmen on the scene of the disaster, arriving in Baton Rouge by 5:00 p.m., just hours after the eye of the hurricane skirted New Orleans. The crews were from Detachment 1717th Medical Company and E Company, 245th Rear ATS (Air Traffic Service).

Before nightfall, the Oklahoma Black Hawks began work. The helicopters landed at the Superdome where chaos reigned. Second Lieutenant Michael Warren, the pilot of one of the Black Hawks, was handed a map and ordered to search a specific area. Warren said, "We didn't have to look very far to find survivors."

The other Black Hawk pilot, CW4 Michael E. Taylor of Noble, said, "People were on rooftops waving t-shirts and towels." It was a hazardous situation for the pilots. Using countless hours of training, they maneuvered the Black Hawks around downed power lines and debris and landed on rooftops that were never designed to support a helicopter. Staff Sergeant Lari Trollinger of Wanette operated the hoist that lowered a medic down to survivors. Often, the pilot was forced to lift the helicopter a few feet so the medic could clear tree branches or broken pieces of buildings. When a medic took a much-needed break, the pilot landed on a sloped roof and the hoist operator carried the evacuees to the hospital.

Lieutenant Colonel Robbie Asher of Oklahoma City received reports that 54 rescues were made, even as darkness descended upon a city without electric power. A dispatch from one crew said, "They are operating within a certain sector, and are basically flying within that sector looking for folks on their roofs. Congested flight pattern makes it a little hairy after dark." Before their mission was completed, the Black Hawk crews rescued 489 people and transported more than 74,000 pounds of food and water.

Black Hawk crews were directed to deliver victims to high ground to be provided food, water, and medical attention and then were transported to shelters. However, poor coordination among local and federal officials resulted in people waiting for hours and days for help. A congressional investigation later found, "The City of New Orleans was unprepared to

help people evacuate, as many buses from the city's own fleet were submerged, while at the same time officials had not arranged in advance for drivers for those buses that were available."

The congressional report also discovered that the New Orleans Fire Department owned no boats and the police department owned only five craft. It was a hodge-podge of privately-owned boats and boats from the Louisiana Department of Fisheries and Wildlife. FEMA did not send buses until two days past landfall. Tens of thousands of people were forced to wait in unspeakably horrible conditions before they were evacuated.

As later analysis of the federal response to Katrina revealed the Department of Homeland Security and FEMA did not involve the National Guard before the storm struck. There were legal reasons why active duty forces could not be used for law enforcement activity, a critical need in New Orleans. That is how and why the National Guard saved the day.

General Wyatt was in constant communication with adjutant generals in other states, Secretary of Homeland Security Michael Chertoff, and Lieutenant General H. Steven Blum, Chief of the National Guard Bureau at the Pentagon. Blum was officially in charge of deployment of the nation's National Guardsmen. It was his responsibility to literally go to the White House to brief President Bush and his staff on a cogent National Guard plan to assist the Gulf States, especially Louisiana. Blum used his influence to cut through a maze of technicality and use federal purchasing authority to support

Major General Robbie Asher, Oklahoma Adjutant General in 2016, was a lieutenant colonel during the Army National Guard's deployment to the Gulf Coast.

People seek high ground as a helicopter lands at the Superdome which was surrounded by water. *Courtesy Oklahoma Publishing Company.*

Katrina survivors wade in waist-deep water to reach the Superdome. *Courtesy FEMA.*

National Guard troops and to provide for direct federal reimbursement of troops that were being activated in active duty status under state authority.

General Blum and Assistant Homeland Security Secretary Paul McHale, Jr., held a joint news conference. It was revealed that the National Guard was exempt from the Posse Comitatus Act, a federal statute enacted by Congress in 1878 that prohibits the use of American active military personnel to enforce laws and domestic policy.

The law resulted in President Rutherford B. Hayes withdrawing federal troops from the former Confederate States of America, officially ending William T. Sherman's March through the South following the Civil War. Secretary McHale told reporters, "We have a critical need for law enforcement in New Orleans because civilian law enforcement is unable to protect the citizens and property. The National Guard is our only answer and they can work side by side with law enforcement officials in ways the active duty forces cannot."

General Blum announced plans to send enough National Guardsmen into New Orleans within three days to quadruple the size of the police departments of the Big Easy and surrounding cities devastated by the hurricane. General Blum said:

The citizen soldiers and airmen are trained professionals. They have the right skill sets. They are military police. Many are civilian law enforcement officers. They come with great expertise and great sensitivity to the fact that they are there in support of existing law enforcement agencies.

The National Guard deployment was the lone bright spot in the nation's emergency response to the devastation left by Hurricane Katrina. The National Guard Bureau cut through red tape by making direct requests for available troops to state adjutant generals. The process ultimately resulted in the largest National Guard deployment in American history, with 50,000 troops from 49 states and two territories.

However, other states were handcuffed. The Texas National Guard had been deployed to help their citizens struck by Katrina and were standing by for other bad weather headed their way. General Wyatt later reflected:

We were in a position to immediately help New Orleans. We were the closest state. We had C-130 cargo aircraft to shuttle troops and supplies. Within a few hours of landfall, when it was safe to fly, we were ready to go.

In New Orleans, crowds topped 30,000 at the Superdome and another 25,000 at the Convention Center. Looting was rampant around the city. Back in Oklahoma, General Wyatt received an urgent request for deployment of CH-47 Chinook helicopters and personnel for security and transport of supplies. Louisiana officials were quick to emphasize that martial law had not been declared, only a "state of emergency" implemented.

A mass of humanity on the floor of the Superdome.

Oklahoma state staff and major unit commands conducted a swift mission analysis. With guidance from the National Guard Bureau, plans were made to deploy a battalion of military police, 50 2.5-ton trucks, and 250 personnel to man the operation. On August 31, General Wyatt issued an order that the Oklahoma National Guard Task Force would be mobilized and deployed to Louisiana within 72 hours.

General Wyatt's directive was specific. The Army National Guard's Quick Reaction Force (QRF), 90th Troop CMD, should be on airplanes headed to the Big Easy within hours. For nearly six months, members of the QRF carried pagers with them, day and night. At 8:40 a.m. on August 31, more than 150 members of the 1345th Transportation Company were notified on their pagers to report to their armories ready for duty. Meanwhile, the 45th Field Artillery Brigade and 160th Field Artillery Battalion were designated as a follow-on force (FOF).

CHAPTER THREE

FIRST BOOTS ON THE GROUND

Streets were blocked by debris and downed power lines. Tree limbs and smashed cars were everywhere. But there was not a soul around. It was eerie, like a scene from a very bad horror movie.

Master Sergeant Byron Fry

The Lockheed C-130 Hercules cargo aircraft, the workhorse of the United States Air Force and the Air National Guard. *Courtesy U.S. Air Force.*

Within two hours of being notified, members of the Quick Reaction Force (QRF) reported and prepared to board C-130 Hercules transport planes operated by the 185th Airlift Squadron and 137th Maintenance Group of the Oklahoma Air National Guard. Because of the potential danger of the mission, each guardsman sent to Louisiana was issued IBAS, a bullet-resistant vest for protection against gunfire.

By 5:00 p.m. that day, the QRF was in place in Louisiana and troops of the 1345th were loaded onto Chinook helicopters and ferried to the Superdome. First Lieutenant Geoff Legler of Norman, with the Oklahoma National Guard Office of Public Affairs, described the scene:

As they circled the dome to land, the smell of death hung in the air and look of desperation on the faces of the thousands of people below was apparent. Never before had these soldiers been exposed to such a grizzly scene. Even Oklahoma Guardsmen who had previously deployed to Afghanistan and Iraq were not fully prepared for what they saw below.

Specialist David Webb of Spencer was shocked by what he saw, "As we touched down, I saw helpless people by the thousands both at the Superdome and stranded on highways and bridges surrounding the dome."

The Oklahoma QRF set up a command post. Because the Superdome was uninhabitable and surrounded by water, Oklahoma Guardsmen established sleeping quarters on the third level of a nearby parking garage. It was late and soldiers were told to get some rest and be prepared to begin a very long day at daybreak.

Lieutenant Colonel Mike Chase of Chandler worked for the 45th Infantry Brigade. He was part of a "torch party," a group of senior guardsmen who were some of the first troops on the ground as an advance team with the QRF to assess the situation and to be able to advise General Wyatt and senior staff on specific needs. Other members of the torch party were Lieutenant Jimmy Thomas of Yukon, an Oklahoma City police officer, and Major Joel Potts of Braggs, designated to serve as liaison with Louisiana authorities. The torch party took satellite phones and alerted superiors to the horror of the disaster scene.

The Black Hawk helicopter has been a reliable aircraft for the U.S. Army and the Army National Guard. It was used for medical evacuation from the Superdome and other locations.

As 27 members of the QRF awoke to a continuing scene of chaos in the blocks around the Superdome in downtown New Orleans, dozens of units of the Oklahoma National Guard prepared in their local armories to either report to Air National Guard bases in Oklahoma City or Tulsa for air transport to Louisiana or to begin the two-day convoy by road. Oklahoma units took so many pieces of equipment to the Gulf Coast, it was necessary to move them by land.

Army National Guard units deployed included the 345th Quartermaster Battalion; 700th Support Battalion; 160th Field Artillery; lst Battalion, 171st Field Artillery; Troop E, 145th Cavalry; lst Battalion, 179th Infantry; lst Battalion, 180th Infantry; lst Battalion, 279th Infantry; 1345th Transportation; Company E, 345 Aviation; Rapid Assessment and Initial Detection (RAID) Team, HHC, 45th Infantry Brigade, and 105th Mobile Public Affairs Detachment.

From the Air National Guard in Oklahoma, units included the 185th Airlift Squadron; 137th Maintenance Group; 137th Medical Group; 137th Aerial Port Squadron; 137th Logistics Readiness Squadron; 13th Service Flight; 137th Aeromedical Evacuation Squadron; 137th Security Forces Squadron; 137th Mission Support Flight; 137th Communications Flight; and the 137th Tanker Airlift Control Element.

When Task Force Commander General Deering arrived on the ground in New Orleans, he could not believe what he saw. He said, "Basically, there's no water, there's no sewer, there's no power. It's like a Third World country. Human suffering is everywhere." General

Looters ran wild in New Orleans before the arrival of the National Guard. *Courtesy Oklahoma Publishing Company.*

Satellite phones were the Guard's only communication in the first days of the mission because land lines and cell phone towers were down.

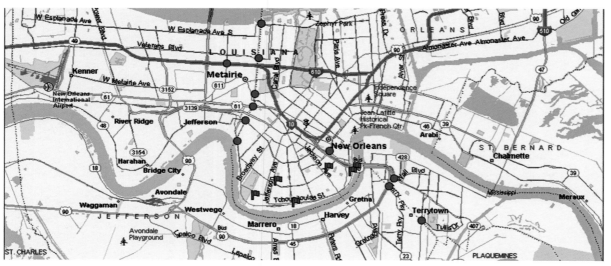

One of the first actions was for the National Guard to establish checkpoints to monitor the flow of traffic into flood-stricken areas.

Deering recognized immediately that it was not just a domestic assistance situation, it was indeed a military operation.

Deering said, "We went to New Orleans with what we had on our backs. We took ten days of supplies and rations and made sure that all maintenance and logistics personnel we would need for the massive job were on their way." There was mass confusion and little communication in a large hangar at the Air National Guard Base at Belle Chasse, a New Orleans suburb in Plaquemines Parish on the west bank of the Mississippi River.

Deering remembered, "It was me with two Humvees and six people trying to figure it all out." The first night, Deering and his staff slept outside on the tarmac. All he could see were airplanes lined up waiting to offload their supplies. It was miserably hot on the ramp during the night and the following day. Deering, self-described as "not a patient man," recognized no one was in control and there was little coordination of hundreds of personnel showing up each hour. Also, he had several Oklahoma units arriving shortly and he did not want them sitting around for long periods of time when there was so much work to be done.

It was apparent to Louisiana National Guard officials that General Deering had the leadership qualities to put some structure into using men and equipment to help people in need. So, he was selected to command a force of more than 15,000 troops in New Orleans, including one active duty brigade each from the 82nd Airborne and the 1st Cavalry Division, two brigades of National Guard troops from other states, and 1,200 troops from the Marine Expeditionary Force.

It was unusual for a National Guard officer to be chosen to head such an operation, but Oklahoma troops were the first on the ground and Louisiana and Department of Defense officials recognized that Oklahoma soldiers were arriving "fast and furious" and were well organized and well-supplied. General Deering's new command was officially labeled "Task Force New Orleans."

Major Tommy Mancino of Norman, in civilian life a dean at the University of Phoenix, was responsible for intelligence for the 45th Infantry Brigade Combat Team. He was present at some of the first meetings that General Deering had with New Orleans Mayor Ray Nagin and the city's police chief, Edwin P. "Eddie" Compass, III.

"General Deering took immediate control of the situation," Mancino remembered. "He walked into a room with the air of authority and local officials knew he had thousands of troops and equipment at his disposal. They looked at him for guidance."

Brigadier General Myles Deering, right, briefs Lieutenant General H. Steven Blum, chief of the National Guard Bureau.

New Orleans Mayor Ray Nagin, right, meets with Oklahoma National Guard officials.

It was a remarkable thing. The week before we were sitting at our civilian jobs as police officers, truck drivers, firemen, bankers, ranchers, farmers, computer experts, and businessmen, and two days later we were sitting on a tarmac in New Orleans getting ready to go and do good things for the people of New Orleans.

Lieutenant Colonel Mike Thompson

Lieutenant Colonel Mike Thompson later was promoted to brigadier general, the first African American general officer in the Oklahoma National Guard and, at the time of publication, served as Oklahoma Commissioner of the Department of Public Safety.

Long meetings with New Orleans officials exposed their lack of ability to handle the disaster. General Deering properly began meetings with, "What we can do to help?" But when Mayor Nagin and Chief Compass could not formulate a cogent request, General Deering and his commanders acted.

Mancino said, "At some of the first meetings we met in a room at the Emergency Operations Center that had a shelf of notebooks filled with disaster and recovery plans that were completely worthless in the present environment." When General Deering left to coordinate with staff back in Oklahoma, Mancino, as a major, was left to give instructions to city staff. "It was no problem for me," he said, "because I knew General Deering would back me up."

Police Chief Compass resigned less than a month after Katrina hit New Orleans. He said he was forced to resign after he was heavily criticized for his leadership after 249 officers, 14 percent of the 1,750-member force, abandoned their posts and refused to report for disaster duty. Compass also was blamed for failing to crack down on later-discovered corruption in the New Orleans Police Department. Compass' resignation was days after an emergency injunction was handed down, prohibiting him and his officers "from confiscating lawfully-possessed firearms from citizens."

Mayor Nagin was criticized nationally by government officials and news media for what they perceived was a lack of leadership during the crisis. In 2014, Nagin was convicted on 21 charges of wire fraud, bribery, and money laundering related to bribes from city contractors before and after Hurricane Katrina and was sentenced to serve a 10-year sentence in federal prison.

Command Sergeant Major Tony Riggs of Norman, lst Battalion, 171st Field Artillery, said Police Chief Compass was upset that National Guard troops were issued only one magazine of ammunition per soldier. "He was irate, out of control," Riggs remembered, "He said this is a war zone and one magazine is not going to get it." Riggs responded, "No sir, I disagree. This is not a war zone. All my soldiers have plenty of ammunition."

From that moment on, Riggs knew the National Guard was on its own and would make appropriate decisions about the use of force. Riggs said, "It did sound like a war zone at night with constant gunfire and sirens. But in the day time, it was a different matter." When Riggs and several of his men arrived at the convention center, people stood up and started applauding. He said, "They knew we were going to help them. They were glad we were there."

"General Deering was the right man for the mission in New Orleans," Major Mancino later reflected. "He has a deep appreciation of the mission of the National Guard and was

Many Oklahoma Air National Guard flights went into Belle Chasse, Louisiana.

Trucks from the 1345th Transportation Company trudge through flood waters.

ANY KIND OF MAP WILL DO

There was a shortage of maps for National Guardsmen for the first few hours and days of the Katrina mission. Some units picked up "visitor's guides" from newsstands outside closed restaurants. Sergeant First Class Joel Wakefield of Chandler stopped at a truck stop on his way into New Orleans and "bought every map he could find." After cleaning out that truck stop, Wakefield repeated his map mission at the next exit. Staff Sergeant Eric Wolf of Owasso grabbed every city map from an abandoned car rental agency. Sharpies were used to mark maps to divide areas of responsibility. From Tulsa, Captain Nate Morgans' unit tore a city map out of a phone book found on the street and used duct tape to attach it to a clipboard.

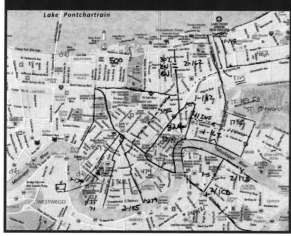

Guard commanders divided the hardest hit areas of New Orleans into sectors.

personally concerned about doing everything we could to help as many people survive the event."

Eighteen hours a day, Deering and his commanders calculated the logistical support needed for the thousands of troops under his command. Basic questions were, with 2,500 soldiers, how many bottles of water does a soldier drink in a day of 90 degrees and 70 percent humidity? Another question posed was how many rations would be needed? Simple math dictated a huge volume of food and water to sustain his troops.

Even though troops from the 82nd Airborne were later deployed to safe, high ground in the French Quarter and received much national news attention, Oklahoma soldiers were the only armed troops that could help stop the chaos. General Wyatt said, "It was ironic. Active duty troops with berets had a lot of guns, but were forbidden by law to load them."

"Welcome to devastation," was the first impression of Lieutenant Colonel Paul Metcalfe of Walters, the follow on force commander, when he and his soldiers entered the Superdome on

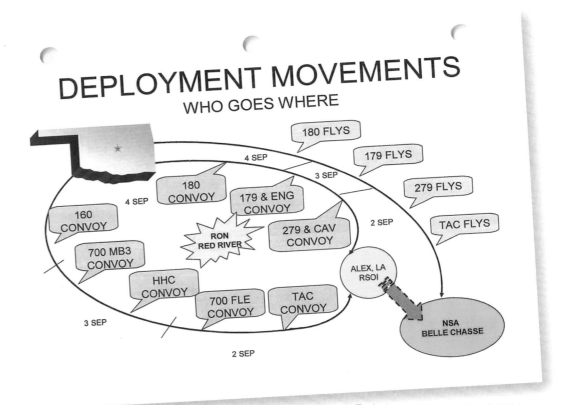

Early troop movements of Oklahoma National Guard units.

September 2. A veteran of 25 years in the military and two overseas deployments, Metcalfe compared the reaction of survivors to battle fatigue.

Lieutenant Colonel Mike Thompson of Edmond will never forget standing on a roof and watching houses burning in the distance and hoping that the flames would burn out before they reached his command post. "The houses were just left to burn," he said, "there was no water in the hydrants for firemen to use to douse the flames."

Soldiers from Headquarters; Headquarters Battery, 45th Field Artillery Brigade; and 1st Battalion, 171st Field Artillery, walked into a tense situation. Metcalfe said, "Immediately we were involved in chaos. There was a huge amount of stress, frustration, and anger, and our job was to create a sense of calm and give hope to the obviously hopeless people."

The first goal was to sustain life and aid those who were injured or ill. Specialist Jeremy Johns of Harrah, a soldier with the 1345th, had been a medic on active duty and volunteered with two Guard medics to help people in the mall area of the Superdome. Many heat-related casualties were treated with IVs. Once people were rehydrated and placed in the shade, most recovered quickly. Trench foot was a common malady for residents who had been exposed to flood waters for days. Johns said, "About one of our five people we saw had trench foot." The only remedy was to find the afflicted a chair and elevate their feet.

For the National Guardsmen, the saddest discovery was the number of children who

suffered from dehydration and other heat-related illnesses. When one mother could not get through the crowd surrounding the medics, desperate to save her baby, she passed the infant over the heads of the crowd toward the medic station.

Medics did not have proper IV catheters for babies so all they could do is to remove the babies' clothing and give them tiny cups of water. As the babies were stabilized, medics handed them to waiting women patients to hold and continue to give water. The most seriously

Oklahoma Army National Guardsmen established security duties throughout New Orleans.

Smoke from fires in New Orleans masks the sun. *Courtesy Oklahoma Publishing Company.*

ill babies were transported by helicopter to hospitals outside the flood-stricken areas.

Guardsmen listened to stories of survivors who witnessed rapes and other crimes. The displaced residents, waiting to be taken to shelters in northern Louisiana and other states, described how the Superdome became "a lawless hellhole beset by rape and murder." The masses of people were dirty, afraid, and exhausted. They pressed their faces against metal gates, pleading for a chance to board a bus and get away from their refuge that had become a nightmare. A newspaper reporter described the situation as a concentration camp with thousands of people emerging like "a slow-moving tide of desperation looking for escape and relief."

People held children and dogs over their heads to keep them from getting crushed. The floors of the stadium were soaked from rain that seeped in through the damaged roof. The pervading stench was a testament to overflowing toilets that forced people to relieve themselves in hallways and stairwells. A handful of policemen were as desperate as those seeking shelter. One police officer was mad at the city government for not providing enough supplies to keep the masses comfortable. The officer said, "You can't be trapped in here for five days without going crazy. People were locked in here like prisoners. There was no ventilation. Old people needed medication and couldn't get it. Bodies were stacked in a freezer that was without power."

A critical situation arose when tens of thousands of people jammed onto the bridge that connected the mall and the arena portion

A CH-47 Chinook helicopter drops water on a fire in New Orleans from a 1,320-gallon "Bambi" bucket.

Setting up communications systems was a priority for early troops in New Orleans.

of the Superdome. Guardsmen were concerned that children, disabled, and elderly people might be crushed if the crowd panicked. Slowly, troops began moving people away from the bridge and entrances to it. Entry control points were set up to keep the crowd on the bridge at a minimum.

Major Joel Potts was on site at the Superdome to serve as liaison to the Louisiana National Guard and to get an on-ground assessment of the situation inside the famous arena. He met with Mayor Nagin and his staff and representatives of the New Orleans Police Department.

Sergeant Phillip Rutz of Okeene said there was tension in the air at the Superdome. "The people were so tense, scared and hungry, it seemed like something could happen anytime. We were able to make a show of force and to make people feel safer because we were there."

A Chinook helicopter from Detachment 1, Company G, 149th Aviation, and its crew helped solve problems at the Superdome. Chief Warrant Officer Carlos Cascante of Choctaw was first told to stay away from the Superdome, but when the situation there remained unstable, the Chinook crew made four trips to carry troops from four different staging areas to manage and help evacuate the survivors. It turned out to be a two-way aid mission. On their first landing with troops at the Superdome, the crew loaded survivors in wheelchairs and took them to safer evacuation locations.

Lieutenant Colonel Mike Thompson, commander of the 1st Battalion, 279th Infantry, led his troops into New Orleans as the first infantry unit to deploy. They arrived days before active duty military personnel were in place. Thompson, Oklahoma's Commissioner of Public Safety in 2016, said, "I remember distinctly seeing the 82nd Airborne show up, get out, straighten their berets, and start walking across the field." Thompson remembered, "Not that it was a competition, but I am very proud of what we were able to do on such a short notice."

The role of the 279th Infantry was to support the local police department, perform search and rescue, and evacuate citizens that remained in the flood zone. Immediately, Thompson was faced with two competing priorities— stop lawlessness and rescue people who were stranded by high water. On one hand, significant looting was being reported and needed to be stopped. The other concern was hundreds of people who could be spotted from overflying aircraft perched on rooftops or hanging onto fence posts.

Alpha Company of the 1st Battalion, 279th Infantry arrived by C-130 at the New Orleans

A week after Katrina hit New Orleans, much of the downtown area still sat under water.

STRANGE SOUNDS

There were many strange sounds for National Guardsmen in New Orleans during the Hurricane Katrina mission. But one of the strangest was reported by Lieutenant Colonel Mike Thompson. At 3:00 a.m. he heard the clippety-clop of what sounded like horses. It was. He looked out and saw about a dozen large horses running down the street. Flood waters obviously had driven them from their pastures or barns.

Soldiers from the Army Guard's 1st Battalion, 279th Infantry exit an Air Guard C-130 in New Orleans.

Naval Air Station. Company Commander, Captain Nate Morgans was first told to set up a giant hangar to receive thousands of evacuees. He and his troops immediately began the task. Then, Louisiana officials changed their minds and said the company was needed at the convention center. Alpha Company loaded onto H-46 Sea Knight helicopters and were transported to the convention center where mass confusion reigned.

A public relations problem for National Guard troops was caused by statements made by Mayor Nagin who went on television and said, "The National Guard is here now and they have machine guns with real bullets. If you loot, they will shoot you." Lieutenant Colonel Thompson did not intend to have his men and women driving around shooting looters. What he envisioned was that the very presence of troops in uniform would "give the folks pause" and serve as a deterrent to looting and other crimes. It was a challenge to choose between the dramatic television statements of the mayor and the calm approach of being present in an area. Thompson said, "We never got the conflicting guidance between the governor and mayor resolved, so we just had to go with what we thought as Oklahomans made sense in that situation."

Mayor Nagin was perceived as wanting the National Guard to "pretty much grab everybody, put them in the back of a five-ton truck, and throw them out of New Orleans." Instead, the Oklahoma Guard came in force, but in peace, and tried to work with what was left of the decimated and worn out New Orleans Police Department. "The police were excited to see us," remembered Lieutenant Colonel Monty Brodt of Oklahoma City, commander of the 1st Battalion, 179th Infantry, headquartered in Stillwater.

Brodt and his staff visited the 2nd District police station looking for guidance. Instead they found officers walking around in mismatched clothing

Oklahoma Army National Guardsmen search door-to-door for survivors.

"This isn't Afghanistan. These are our fellow citizens.
You've got to look at it as if this was your brother or sister or family."

Lieutenant Colonel Monty Brodt of Oklahoma City,
commander of the 1st Battalion, 179th Infantry, headquartered in Stillwater

Flood waters inundated 80 percent of New Orleans. *Courtesy* New Orleans Times-Picayune.

with uniforms hanging on makeshift lines to dry. When Brodt arrived at the office of the captain in charge, they found a man who could not help them. "He just looked exhausted," Brodt said, "We told him we had 400 troops who could help if he would tell us what to do. He was overwhelmed and didn't have a plan." Finally, it was decided that Brodt's unit would provide security in the Garden District, an area of upscale homes.

The police captain told Brodt to use any building that was available and, "if you find any looters, just shoot them. We will take care of the crap." It was the second time that day that Oklahoma Guard officers had been told to shoot looters on sight. Brodt was offended by the officer's suggestion. He said, "This isn't Afghanistan. These are our fellow citizens. You've got to look at it as if this was your brother or sister or family. More importantly, you don't want to have anything that will haunt you for the rest of your life."

Army guardsmen stand at the edge of a flooded New Orleans neighborhood.

Air National Guardsmen load gear of Army guardsmen for the flight from Oklahoma to Louisiana.

CHAPTER FOUR

AIR SUPPORT AND LONG CONVOYS

The Oklahoma National Guard's professional and efficient response to Hurricane Katrina testifies of the great collaborative effort between citizen soldiers from the Army and Air sides—all with one mission, to help our neighbors who were desperate for help.

Colonel Mike McCormick, Commander
137th Airlift Wing

National Guard troops poured into New Orleans to restore order, protect property, and rescue survivors after almost a week of near anarchy. Having largely emptied the Superdome, which had become a squalid pit of misery and violence, National Guardsmen turned their attention to the convention center, where people waited to be evacuated as corpses rotted in the streets.

The Louis Armstrong International Airport served as a massive clearing house for some of the sickest victims of Katrina and elderly patients from nursing homes and the Veterans Administration Hospital that needed transport to other states. Inside four triage tents at the airport, medical personnel helped people who had gone for days without regular medication.

From all over Oklahoma, Guardsmen began deploying to New Orleans. Bill Secrest of Seiling, and his sons, John of Seiling, and Travis of Yukion, reported to the armory in Alva as Bravo Company, 1st Battalion, 179th

Infantry was activated. The last active duty for the unit was in Iraq. Specialist Vanessa Thomas left her three daughters with her mother and left with more than 200 troops from the 23rd Street Armory in Oklahoma City. Boxes of food and water and troops armed with M-16 rifles and dressed in green fatigues loaded into High Mobility Multipurpose Wheeled Vehicles, commonly called a Humvee, a four-wheel drive military light truck that supplanted the role of the traditional jeep in the military.

The 171st Field Artillery Brigade sent 350 soldiers to provide fueling for hundreds of civilian and military vehicles employed in the search and rescue effort. In the first two weeks of the mission, the ten 2,500-gallon trucks of the 171st delivered more than 155,000 gallons of

GRAZING HERD—RAGING BULL

The 180th Infantry Battalion had a unique method of notifying soldiers. They used a code. If it was a rehearsal notification, the words "Grazing Herd" were used. However, if it was the real thing, the soldier on the other end of the line heard the words, "Raging Bull," and knew it was a real emergency and to pack his or her stuff and be at the assigned armory within an allotted time frame.

Long convoys transported troops and equipment to the Gulf Coast.

diesel fuel. Sergeant Michael Bone of Lawton said, "We delivered fuel to police stations, fire houses, pump stations, and emergency centers." Fuel was shipped into New Orleans by Navy tankers then offloaded by civilian contractors for delivery to the 171st.

A small cooking unit from the Mangum Armory had less than 12 hours' notice to say goodbye to their families and notify their employers of their deployment to Louisiana. As they left town with their trucks packed with M-16 rifles, tents, fuel, and rations, they also carried boxes of water and groceries donated by Mangum businesses. Twenty vehicles carried 57 guardsmen from Elk City and Clinton headed for the Big Easy. Sergeant Gary Nix of Elk City said every truck attached to the armory would be part of the convoy to New Orleans.

Specialist Richard Kerr of Reydon, assigned to the Headquarters Battery, 45th Field Artillery, in Enid, kissed his wife goodbye, arrived at the armory for a briefing, and headed out 30 minutes later in a convoy of two five-ton trucks.

The tail of an Oklahoma Air National Guard C-130.

Their goal was to get to New Orleans before the rest of the unit arrived by airlift. After Kerr and Sergeant First Class Joe Salinas of Purcell arrived at Fort Sill, they joined other units on their way to New Orleans. Kerr said, "All at once, instead of being a two-person convoy, we became a 110-vehicle convoy."

As the convoy drove through Dallas, sirens from police cars and motorcycles screamed, making it easier for slower military trucks to get through otherwise crowded traffic. In the back of trucks were rations and water for ten days and racks of M-16 rifles.

Five days into Task Force Oklahoma, Oklahoma National Guard units sent 272 Humvees, 47 trailers, 54 two-and-a-half ton trucks, 110 five-ton trucks, eight dump trucks, and 23 ambulances to support troops in New Orleans.

Units from the 137th Airlift Wing, located at Will Rogers Air National Guard Base in Oklahoma City, began around-the-clock operations to assist Army National Guard partners. Colonel W. Emery Fountain of Norman , deputy chief of staff operations, called it a symbiotic relationship between the Army and Air Guard. "One makes the other better," he said.

Colonel Mike McCormick of Piedmont and Colonel Greg Ferguson of Norman, commander and vice commander of the 137th Airlift Wing at Will Rogers Air National Guard Base in Oklahoma City, directed the air support for Task Force Oklahoma. C-130s from the 137th Airlift Squadron and the 185th Airlift Squadron delivered more than 2,100 soldiers, government officials, and civilian aid workers, and nearly 700 tons of cargo to assist the Army National Guard. They flew 48 missions and 159 sorties. Amazingly, they executed 100 percent of their assigned sorties with an on-time rate of 98.7 percent.

The Air Guard deployment came just months after the Base Realignment and Closure Commission (BRAC), the congressionally-mandated reassessment of Department of Defense bases, announced plans for the 137th to transition from the airlift business and lose its coveted C-130's. In 1979, the wing was the first Air National Guard unit in the nation to receive brand new Lockheed C-130 aircraft. Colonel Ferguson said, "The wing was going through some difficult days. We still had aircraft deployed in Iraq and we were about to lose our airplanes and several units."

When Adjutant General Wyatt contacted Air Guard commanders to transport the QRF, the Air Guard immediately called for volunteers to man flight crews for the four C-130's available. A flight crew normally consisted of two pilots, a navigator, a flight engineer, and a loadmaster. In a complicated cargo mission, often two loadmasters were assigned. Chief Master Sergeant Kirk Brinegar of Bethany, the supervising flight engineer for the C-130s based at Will Rogers, said, "Basically, everybody volunteered. All 22 flight engineers on the roster made themselves available."

Many Air Guard pilots flew commercial airliners in their civilian jobs. Immediately after a national emergency was declared, every major

airline supported activation of its National Guard pilots. Colonel Boone Browning of Oklahoma City, Air Operations Officer, began putting together flight schedules to support the expected heavy demand for delivery of personnel and

Colonel Greg Ferguson, vice commander, 137th Airlift Wing, Oklahoma Air National Guard.

supplies to the Gulf Coast. For the first few days of the Air Guard operation, there were too many volunteers for air crews. However, as crew members came in for needed rest, other volunteers took their place.

The C-130 was a perfect aircraft for operations

such as Task Force Oklahoma. It could land almost anywhere on short 3,000-foot runways, even on dirt strips. The aircraft also was capable of dropping heavy equipment or supplies through its open door and ramp.

Colonel Ferguson was in command of the crew that delivered the QRF to the scene of the disaster. Major airfields were closed, so the Oklahoma C-130 landed on a short airfield on the north side of Lake Pontchartrain. It was dark all around the airfield, so Air Guard crews had to use night vision goggles. Ferguson said, "Because we were operating on a governor-to-governor request, there was no bureaucratic maze of authority to go through. We actually fell into a comfortable operational rhythm to which we had become accustomed the previous two years in combat in the desert."

"We brought all our assets and expertise together with the Army to make Task Force Oklahoma work," Colonel Ferguson said. Air Guard personnel were dispatched to the National Guard Joint Operations Center to run 24-hour-a-day operations. Lieutenant Colonel Ken Carmichael of Edmond received requests from his Army counterpart to transport specific personnel and cargo to Louisiana. Then, Air Guard staff began the task of matching load requirements with airplanes.

Having an Air Guard officer present at the Task Force headquarters paid dividends. Master Sergeant Stephen Rosebrook of Mustang, in charge of training for the 137th Aerial Port Squadron, said, "Having someone in headquarters that knew our capabilities was

Air National Guard loadmasters take a break in the shade while waiting for their next load of cargo headed for the Gulf Coast.

We are really good at what we do—both blue and green in the National Guard. We are a tool in the tool box of the Governor in domestic situations and our neighbors when tragedy strikes.

Master Sergeant Stephen Rosebrook

very important. If Colonel Carmichael didn't know the answer to a question, he knew who to call. From the time a logistical question was formulated to the time it was answered was a very small amount of time."

As Guardsmen were activated, members of the 137th Medical Group administered hundreds of vaccinations to 45th Infantry Division soldiers at the Sand Springs Armory, the Tulsa Air National Guard Base, the Will Rogers Air National Guard Base, and at a staging center in Alexandria, Louisiana.

The 137th Aeromedical Evacuation Squadron was the first National Guard unit to arrive on the Gulf Coast to evacuate patients from hospitals without power and under water. One of the first

C-130s to arrive at the New Orleans commercial airport for the purpose of evacuating patients from the New Orleans Veterans Administration Hospital (VA) was piloted by Captain Jason Rozneck of Edmond. When the plane landed, he saw at least 1,000 people on stretchers that FEMA supplied for the emergency evacuation of patients.

Captain Keith Reed of Tecumseh was the medical crew director for the 137th Air Medical Evacuation Squadron and aboard the first Oklahoma airplane to arrive. There was no power at the airport and all commercial flights were canceled. The medical crew, made up of two flight nurses and three medical technicians, began walking through dark corridors looking for the VA patients. Reed said, "We were inundated with people asking us to take patients."

The airport was overrun with injured and sick people trying to get out of the hurricane-stricken city. Reed looked out into an area where patients were being dropped off and saw ambulances three rows deep "as far as the eyes could see." Lines of people were waiting to be identified. Through a sketchy cellphone conversation, Reed learned that the VA patients were still stranded by water. Not wanting to waste a trip, Reed received permission to haul any patients that needed to be evacuated.

Reed and his team began handwriting manifests for people they could help. He said, "There were no medical records and barely any history. We just tried to move them as quickly as possible." Because there was no tower support at the airport, Reed's team and another Aero-Med

Members of the 1st Battalion, 180th Infantry, load onto a C-130 for transport to New Orleans.

Members of the Air Guard's 137th Aero Med Squadron wait to transfer injured evacuees at Will Rogers Air National Guard Base.

team on another Oklahoma C-130 began loading patients quickly because the aircraft needed to depart before nightfall. Ambulances drove completely around the airport to the rear of the tarmac where the C-130s were parked.

That is when training and previous experience took over. Oklahoma Air Guard crews had to be creative to move patients confined to a litter. They commandeered airline baggage trailers and filled them with litters. Then, a tug was used to pull several trailers in a "train" to the aircraft.

In the crisis mode, crews took patients blindly.

Reed said, "We saw all kinds of issues. Most of them didn't really know what was going on. They didn't have their medication, they were dirty, smelly, hungry, and thirsty. For those in great pain, we comforted with pain medication."

When the C-130s departed New Orleans, they had no idea where they were taking patients. However, once in the air, Red Cross officials made arrangements for the two aircraft loads of victims to be flown to Houston, Texas. When the Oklahoma crews arrived in Houston, ambulances were lined up for a quarter mile to

take the evacuees to area hospitals.

Nurses and medical technicians in the Aero-Med unit had deployed many times. They had evacuated wounded from combat zones in Afghanistan and Iraq. The unit could be deployed independently of aircraft, but in Task Force Oklahoma, their fellow Air Guardsmen supported their efforts with C-130s from Will Rogers.

Wing Commander McCormick flew one of the first two sorties to evacuate VA Hospital patients who finally were able to be transported to the New Orleans airport. Litters of patients

A line of ambulances await arrival of evacuees from New Orleans for transfer to Oklahoma City area hospitals.

A RANCID ODOR

After two weeks of non-stop flying into New Orleans, when we descended through about 2,000 feet, the smell that came into the cockpit was just rancid. It was the rot that was left over from the wake of the hurricane.

Captain Jason Rozneck

lined the interior of the C-130 with flight nurses and technicians closely monitoring them. Aero-Meds configured the back of the aircraft to accommodate ambulatory patients and those who needed to stay horizontal. McCormick said, "Sometimes it was a two-hour process to reconfigure. It's a pretty dramatic transformation from the back of an airplane if it had been set up just for seats for passengers."

From the airport in New Orleans, McCormick flew patients to Will Rogers. Again, the National Guard performed quickly and efficiently. McCormick said, "The VA had approached Tinker Air Force Base to receive patients, but the bureaucracy of the Air Force prevented someone from saying, 'Just bring them on.'" When McCormick, as wing commander, was approached, his immediate answer was, "We will be ready to receive them."

As each of about a half dozen sorties landed at Will Rogers with from 20 to 40 patients aboard, nurses and technicians met patients in a hangar quickly cleaned out and turned into a triage area. From there, patients were carried by ambulance to the Oklahoma City VA Hospital or a half dozen public hospitals in the area.

After the initial medical evacuation flights of Oklahoma C-130s, 10 members of the 137th Aero-Meds were deployed to the Armstrong Airport, flown there with a deuce and a half and supplies by a C-130 from Missouri. Once on the ground, the Air Guardsmen began working eight hours on, eight hours off. Reed's teams screened thousands of patients, assigned wheelchairs and litters, and then took them to a concourse in

preparation to load onto waiting aircraft.

Because the jet ways designated for commercial aircraft were being used to exit the terminal, a lot of ingenuity was necessary to move patients down to the ground. They used baggage conveyor belts. Four personnel would take a litter to the end of the jet way and hand it off to two crew members who could walk down the narrow baggage belt to two feet from the ground. Another waiting team picked up the litter and hoisted it onto the airplane.

Many civilian volunteers, men and women and teenagers, helped move patients. For heavy patients, that was a problem, until Reed and his crew began using stainless steel tables normally used at security checkpoints. They duct-taped legs of two tables together and made an efficient transportation system of "gurneys" to transport litters.

Crews were focused on moving patients through the system. Tech Sergeant Yvonne Whitaker-Payne of Edmond was trying to get through a crowd of people with a litter and was shouting, "Make a hole! Make a hole!" She bumped into Secretary of Defense Donald Rumsfeld who was at the airport surveying the situation. Whitaker-Payne was so focused, she did not realize who Rumsfeld was. However, Rumsfeld understood the situation, jumped out of the way, and shouted, "Hey, get out of their way! Let them do their job!"

On another occasion during the seven days that the Oklahoma team was on the ground at the airport, former Vice President Al Gore arrived with a chartered aircraft and announced he had room for 180 ambulatory patients. Air Guardsmen quickly found 180 patients who could walk or easily be transferred to an airline seat. A quarter of the aircraft ended up being loaded with patients who normally would be on a litter. Captain Reed had to load a double amputee onto a narrow wheelchair that could be pulled down the middle aisle of the aircraft.

One early flight out of New Orleans headed for Oklahoma City was full of patients evacuated from a nursing home that was flooded. Master Sergeant Stephen Rosebrook received short notice that the aircraft was inbound. He put out a call to guardsmen, hospitals, ambulance services—anyone—who could help care for the elderly passengers on the C-130. Rosebrook later described the response:

So many different kinds of uniforms was unbelievable. So many firemen, emergency medical personnel, nurses—people in uniform came to help. I will never forget the picture in my mind of Oklahomans in the middle of their rotations at local hospitals or from the back of an ambulance who answered the call. It was amazing.

Civilian supply lines were cut off by flood waters and much of the Army's rolling stock was in place, so thousands of deployed guardsmen were almost entirely dependent upon the 137th for the first three weeks of service. Each C-130 crew spent 16 hours per day loading supplies, flying to Louisiana, unloading, and flying back to Oklahoma. In the first 96 hours, Oklahoma moved more than 2,000 troops to Louisiana by air and ground.

"Seamless cooperation" were the words used by Major Johnathon Benton of Mustang, who scheduled flights and coordinated air transportation at Joint Force Headquarters. Benton urged the Army to use the Air Guard to their maximum capacity and efficiency. He said, "Our personnel are very anxious to do all that they possibly can, working around the clock to keep troops and supplies moving to the area."

The first mission for Air Operations Officer Browning was to fly to Ada to pick up Army Guardsmen for delivery to the Naval Air Station in New Orleans. When the C-130 landed, it looked "like a zoo" to Browning. He said, "Everyone was leaving their engines running because there was no time on the ramp to shut them off and restart them."

Every few seconds a helicopter flew over the airport. Forklifts ran to and fro, off-loading supplies. Troops filed out of aircraft in masses.

Injured and ill evacuees were transported on stretchers down jetways and onto freight tugs at the New Orleans airport.

When Browning was cleared to take off for the return trip to Oklahoma, a helicopter flew not more than 100 feet above the runway. Browning said, "It was nerve wracking, but fairly well orchestrated."

Flights in and out of New Orleans were during the daylight only. The hurricane knocked out navigation guidance systems which normally could bring airplanes in for landing even in the darkest of nights. With pilots using traditional visual flight rules (VFR) methods, and without a landing system, it was necessary to look for landmarks such as rivers and towns to navigate their way into either New Orleans International Airport or the airport at Belle Chasse.

Captain Jason Rozneck said it was "old school" VFR flying like in World War II. A Navy E2 aircraft was in contact with arriving and departing aircraft. Using a Tactical Pilots Chart, Rozneck and other pilots and navigators teamed up to develop a course to the airport. Once on the ground, Air Force combat controllers riding on ATV's helped direct aircraft to parking areas.

Back in Oklahoma City, the entire base got together and volunteered for duty. Browning remembered, "They would fly the mission, load, or do whatever they needed to do. Everyone wanted to help." Mechanics repaired planes when they needed it and maintenance was performed in the middle of the night.

Loading aircraft was a major task for Air Guard personnel. Staff Sergeant Joseph Connell of Oklahoma City was in charge of running cargo operations at Will Rogers Air National Guard Base. When he received lists of cargo and personnel to be flown to New Orleans, his crew developed a load plan, deciding exactly the weight of cargo and soldiers that could be safely carried on one of the C-130 aircraft. Tech Sergeant Rex Sollers of Oklahoma City was attached to the Air Guard squadron that handled loading and unloading of aircraft on the ramp. As primary load team chief, he directed the efforts of a crew of three to five to load cargo on pallets into the C-130 and assist soldiers in boarding the aircraft.

Around the clock, for nearly 30 days, the Aerial Port Squadron provided up to a dozen men and women for each shift. A small team configured and arranged equipment and supplies onto pallets in a large parking lot. A grid yard with a numbering system and code allowed the crews to know exactly how much each pallet weighed and what its dimensions were. Sergeant Connell said, "Once the pallets were built, we gave the information to a load planner who could look at the list and determine the priority of shipment."

Once crews loaded a few airplanes, the task got easier. Sergeant Sollers said, "We got into a pretty good rhythm knowing each other and how we could work as a team to get planes loaded as quickly as possible. Sometimes we got one plane loaded as another C-130 was landing to refuel and pick up another load."

Ten years after Katrina, Chief Master Sergeant Brinegar reflected:

Katrina wasn't anything different than we had been doing during the war. We fly airplanes and make sure we get the people there and bring them back. That is what we are trained to do. The only thing unique about Katrina was that our location was different. We were in our home country and helping our neighbors.

Whether it was evacuating hospital patients or loading supplies for delivery to the Gulf Coast, it was a 24-hour-a-day operation at Will Rogers in Oklahoma City. Colonel McCormick said, "The clock didn't mean anything to them. Whatever it took to get an airplane ready at any hour of the day or night, they did without question or complaint. I once went there at midnight and there were mechanics on the line on stands turning wrenches on engines."

A morale booster for the Air Guard working around the clock was a 2:00 a.m. visit one morning from General Wyatt. He not only wanted to show his appreciation for the efforts of the men and women working all night, he brought fresh coffee for the troops.

Colonel Philip Abshere of Edmond, a dentist assigned to the 137th Medical Group, and later Air National Guard Surgeon General for

Dentistry, spent two weeks with Joint Task Force Katrina Expeditionary Medical Support at the New Orleans Naval Air Station in Belle Chasse, providing dental care for active duty and National Guard troops and using dental forensics to identify victims.

The 137th Logistics Readiness Squadron coordinated storage and airlift distribution with emergency management officials for the movement of 43,000 gallons of bottled water to Katrina-stricken areas. The 137th Service Flight lodged a base population of 5,000 Army and Air Force personnel and displaced military families at the Gulfport Combat Readiness Training Center in Mississippi. In two tent cities and existing, undamaged facilities, 17 members of the flight provided up to 16,000 meals per day.

Senior Airman Nancy Prykryl of Oklahoma City, a cook for the squadron, said, "Our main focus was to provide morale for the soldiers and airmen. There was no electricity or running water at first. It was hot, dry, stressful, and miserable working 12-hour shifts." Senior Airman and cook Arlene Nilkumhang of Midwest City was a college student at Rose State College and had been in the National Guard only a few months when deployed to Gulfport. She said, "We cooked like crazy. We always wanted to provide a hot meal instead of the troops eating another MRE." The hot meals came from boiling pre-packaged bags of food in water.

Nilkumhang and other deployed soldiers slept outside on cots to avoid the heat in buildings to which power had been interrupted. The lack of a fresh water supply was a disadvantage. They washed their uniforms at night and used bobby pins to hang them on makeshift clotheslines, hopeful that the night air would dry them. "Otherwise," Nilkumhang said, "we wore wet uniforms the next day." Other units of the 137th were sent to England Air Force Base, Louisiana, and Sheppard Air Force Base, Texas.

Working together in tough conditions had a positive impact upon members of the 137th. Nilkumhang said, "When you are in tough scenarios, you build your group closer together. I was new and made friends for life."

The Air Guard's 137th Tanker Airlift Control Element worked with the Aerial Port Squadron (APS) to establish shelter, showers, and electricity for personnel deployed to the area. APS personnel directed all phases of aerial port operations, from processing cargo and providing ramp services to providing mobile air terminal services and support to airlift forces into high threat areas. Later, after the initial response to Katrina, the Air Guard's 219th Engineering and Installation Squadron helped rewire the Louisiana National Guard headquarters decimated by flood waters from the levee breaks in New Orleans.

The 137th Communications Flight sent personnel to provide computer and network support to several active duty and National Guard units at Belle Chasse. There, they set up 24-hour support for operations and put more than 500 computers in Department of Defense compliance, reestablished backup capability, and provided multimedia specialists to document joint operations. The Communications Flight provided invaluable assistance in computerizing activation orders and travel orders to provide accountability and show fiscal responsibility of resources.

For all Air Guardsmen involved in the Hurricane Katrina mission, there was a sense of great accomplishment and solidified members of units. Master Sergeant Adam Cline said:

I usually saw other members of the unit only once a month and on summer training, but when you work 15 hours a day side-by-side with somebody every day, you are hungry and they are hungry and you take care of each other. We got a lot closer. We felt good about what we were doing so there were no arguments or disagreements. It brought my unit much closer together.

An aerial view of Camp Wally Mart in the parking lot of a looted Walmart store.

CHAPTER FIVE

HOME AWAY FROM HOME

We had to set up bases of operation at the first decent place we could find. Oklahoma Guard units worked out of a Walmart parking lot, a fancy restaurant, a Catholic school, a zoo, a warehouse, and even a building once used as an insane asylum.

Sergeant Major Steven Jensen

Looters ransacked the Walmart on Tchoupitoulas Street before guardsmen arrived to make the parking lot their headquarters.

Once National Guard troops were on the ground in New Orleans, the first priority was to set up a base of operations for each unit—a place where soldiers could sleep, eat, and be briefed on their next day's mission. It was hot at night, and hotter all day. The food included Meals Ready to Eat (MRE) and all the warm water you could drink.

New Orleans Police Department officials told National Guard commanders they could use any vacant building, city or state property, or privately-owned parking lots. Such free reign to use basically all flooded areas of the Big Easy made commanders a little uneasy, so units selected a home away from home with respect for owners and nearby occupants. Task Force Orleans Commander General Deering said, "We were not going to occupy any building unless we had the explicit permission of the building owner."

The first base of operation for the Quick Reaction Force was the third floor of a parking garage near the Superdome. Command Sergeant Major Tony Riggs said it was hard to call the space "sleeping quarters" because the soldiers had to lay on concrete. "It was some of the most horrid conditions I had ever been in," Riggs said. There were no sleeping bags or blankets. When he asked for the restroom, he was told to walk down until he found water. There was none, the sewer system was flooded, so he was "on his own." MREs and bottled water were available on site, but no other comforts of home were "anywhere in sight."

Some members of the 279th Infantry based in Vinita moved five times during their mission, sleeping in an apartment complex parking lot, a rundown motel, two area hospitals, and the New Orleans Convention Center.

Military police and decontamination units of Headquarters and Headquarters Company, 45th Infantry Brigade, were among the first soldiers to settle in the parking lot of a Walmart store on Tchoupitoulas Street in Orleans Parish. Tchoupitoulas is the closest major street to the Mississippi River. The store had been looted and guardsmen guarded the facility against arson.

The parking lot was fondly called "Camp Wally Mart" by soldiers. Soon, hundreds of guardsmen operated out of the parking lot. Because General Deering had his headquarters there, many VIPs frequented Camp Wally Mart. The parking lot was centrally located, a few blocks from the convention center, and not far from the Superdome.

The major disadvantage of the parking lot was the heat. General Deering said, "When you're planted there 24 hours a day and 12 of those are under the sunshine with 90 degrees and 70 percent humidity, it becomes miserable." Another problem was anchoring tents in the parking lot for troops to sleep in. Fortunately, an adjacent business loaned the Guard heavy iron anchors and a boring machine to cut through the asphalt. After the mission ended, the anchors were returned "in good order."

Major Scott Houck said the parking lot was "the hottest place I ever was in my whole life." Houck learned a valuable lesson the first night sleeping outside Walmart. He laid his pants on the ground as he slept and a company of fire ants took them over. The next morning, Houck slipped on his pants and began yelling as fire ants began attacking his legs. The pants came off quickly and Houck learned to never lay his pants on the ground again.

When the 45th first arrived in New Orleans, communication was spotty at best. There were no landlines and cell phone service was degraded. General Deering carried three different cell phones from three different providers to improve his chances that one was usable.

To improve communications, Sergeant First

A chapel service in the yard of a residence for the 1st Battalion, 179th Infantry.

Class Vic Roman of Edmond used a "homemade" trailer that he and several automation specialists in the Army Guard converted into a command and control center. The trailer was given to Oklahoma during deployments after Desert Storm to allow family members to call their loved ones from a local armory. Roman and others acquired satellite communications equipment with extra money in the Guard budget.

With the help of the 63rd Civil Support Team, Roman and his group placed the trailer in the

It was the Super Bowl of domestic response. I cannot think of another event in which the National Guard was engaged to that degree for that length of time.

Lieutenant Colonel Mike Chase

Walmart parking lot and gave commanders greatly improved communication by internet and telephone. General Deering said, "It was great when I saw that blue truck pulling up with the civil support team, able to install computer banks so we could communicate with the Joint Operations Center in Oklahoma City."

Roman and his crew, Sergeant First Class Ed Nielson of Luther and Sergeant Joe Funck of Edmond, had computers in several rooms and made video conferencing possible in another

room. General Deering and other commanders were able to video conference with state headquarters for a situational update each day.

The communications trailer was such a hit, Roman and his men were inundated with requests from other commanders. Major Joel Potts called Roman in the middle of the night to request a high frequency radio. Major Tommy Mancino wanted a satellite feed into his tent so he could gather intelligence, especially monitoring local television stations back on the air.

The trailer also had recreational value for the troops after long shifts exposed to dirty water and sweltering conditions. Roman used the television capability from DIRECTV and placed a projector on the top of a ladder to project the picture on the side of the white trailer. It was like an old outdoor movie theater, allowing troops to watch football games and other sporting events.

Showering was a luxury not available to Oklahoma National Guardsmen for the first ten days of the mission to New Orleans. Some troops did not get a shower for two and a half weeks. A "shower" at the Walmart parking lot involved taking large water cans and disappearing behind a trailer or tent along the perimeter. Major Louis Wilham of Edmond, 345th Quartermaster Battalion, described the operation:

A shower at Camp Wally consisted of going to the edge of the parking lot with a jug of water and tip the jug of water over your head. Hopefully, you had a little privacy for your spit bath. It was so hot, it was like a warm shower.

Debris cleanup was a big part of the mission for many Oklahoma Army National Guardsmen.

An Oklahoma Army National Guard truck moves through flood waters.

Next door to the Walmart was a brick warehouse where hundreds of soldiers bunked. It was mostly abandoned, had a tin roof, and was hot. But, it beat huddling under an 18-wheeler to escape the sun as they did when they first arrived in the stricken city.

De La Salle High School housed National Guard members.

The looted Walmart contained medical supplies needed by units in the field. Following General Deering's order, "Don't take anything unless you have permission," commanders contacted Walmart headquarters and obtained permission to take anything from the store. Believing in accountability, Sergeant Major Steven Jensen of Harrah kept meticulous records of what the Guard took so Walmart could be reimbursed. Later Walmart officials thanked the 45th for saving what they could of the property and protecting it from further destruction.

After two weeks of enduring heat rising from the asphalt parking lot, Roman went with brigade officers to look at De La Salle High School, a private Catholic school on St. Charles Avenue in Uptown New Orleans. The school was not damaged by the hurricane so Lieutenant Colonel Mike Chase contacted the president of the local school board and the headmaster of the school. They worked out a deal—troops could live anywhere on the property, except in classrooms, in exchange for providing 24-hour security for the school property.

As electric power came back on, the school water system was operational and soldiers were told they could shower in the school gymnasium. However, medical units arrived and prohibited use of the showers because the water was contaminated. Fortunately, none of the soldiers who took showers became ill. It was back to gallon jugs for showers unless soldiers could sneak to the waterfront along the Mississippi River and use showers set up by FEMA. National Guard troops installed water purification

Soldiers from the 160th Field Artillery set up headquarters at the Riverwalk, an exclusive shopping area along the Mississippi River.

LUXURIOUS LIVING ON THE USS *IWO JIMA*

After Katrina made landfall, the United States Navy sent its new amphibious assault ship, the USS *Iwo Jima*, up the Mississippi River to New Orleans to provide disaster relief and serve as the central command center for federal operations. It was the only functional air field for helicopter operations for days and provided hot meals, showers, and water to thousands of National Guardsmen. The ship also had a full-service first aid and surgical medical operator for disaster victims, guardsmen, and relief workers. President Bush landed on the ship when he visited New Orleans.

The USS *Iwo Jima* at the New Orleans pier.

When Oklahoma Guardsmen discovered the luxurious service available on the *Iwo Jima*, they made their way to the docked ship. Specialist Richard Kerr said, "Some guys ate all three meals on the ship and then went back at midnight for a snack." On the morning President Bush arrived, three Oklahoma Guardsmen were eating breakfast when the President sat down and thanked them for their service.

systems that allowed FEMA to purify water directly from the river.

At the school, Major Scott Houck became a "travel agent" as he began shuttling Guardsmen to and from New Orleans for personal reasons, mostly tied to school attendance. As classes began, he made arrangements for at least a dozen soldiers a day to return to Oklahoma.

Houck also was in charge of distributing mail to Oklahoma units as the search and rescue and recovery phases of the mission slowed somewhat. He and his team drove to Belle Chasse each morning to pick up mail. Sergeant Christina Matlock-Golinghorst of Blanchard and Houck sorted the mail and delivered it to other units. So much mail was arriving, it sometimes took two hours in a tent "in the sweltering heat" sorting mail.

Very few bathrooms in the flooded areas of New Orleans worked in the days after Katrina hit. It is left to history's imagination how more than 2,000 Oklahoma National Guardsmen attended to basic needs. Then, porta-potties began appearing at various encampments. No one really knew where they came from, although it was suspected that many were moved from construction sites in the area.

The problem was that the porta-potties had not been serviced. Major Wilham began developing a plan to clean out the porta potties and provide basic shower and laundry facilities at each unit location. Second Lieutenant Shawn Woolley's brother lived in New Orleans and Woolley, of Oklahoma City, knew the Crescent City "like the back of his hand." Woolley traveled to areas outside the Ninth Ward and hired

companies to immediately begin cleaning out porta-potties. Wilham said, "A cheer came from the soldiers when the disposal truck made a service call and clean toilets were again available."

As the water receded, National Guard trucks more easily navigated the flooded streets.

The delivery of ice was also a logistical problem solved by the 345th. Major Wilham contracted with ice companies in outlying areas to make daily deliveries to checkpoints, battalion locations, and company headquarters. There was plenty of water available for the troops, but ice was needed to

During down time, guardsmen read and played cards. Hurricane Katrina had knocked out television stations.

base of operations in a restaurant that was part of the Culinary Institute of New Orleans. The restaurant was made from an original piece of the Eiffel Tower in Paris, France, and was encased in glass. The restaurant was elevated, so any additional flooding would not affect troops in temporary residence there.

"The only problem," remembered Staff Sergeant Eric Wolf, operations sergeant for the unit's Headquarters Company, "was anytime you are in a building encased in glass in New Orleans in September, with no air conditioning, it's like living in a microwave." The building was "unspeakably hot," but the hurricane knocked out a few windows that provided a breeze in some parts of the building. When power was restored, the restaurant was an ideal location. It was such a nice building, it was a popular place for VIPs and other relief workers. Sergeant Wolf said, "We had the coolest building and the best coffee in town."

There was a reason they had the best coffee. The Culinary Institute was located next door to the offices of the Louisiana Department of Tourism that had a warehouse full of "community coffee," a really good flavor of Louisiana-style coffee. Wolf made the special coffee in huge cauldrons from the restaurant. He said, "One night the FBI came by and liked it so much, they came by every night."

A few days after the power came on, guardsmen began eating better. Harrah's Casino in the French Quarter used staff and volunteers to make thousands of cheeseburgers each day. Soldiers and volunteer workers could

cool it down. The Guard made use of thousands of donated gallon jugs of water, but Wilham said, "It was necessary to cool the water to entice troops to drink plenty of it to stay hydrated."

The 1st Battalion, 279th infantry found a unique

Before troops could be housed in the New Orleans Convention Center, piles of trash had to be removed from the outside and inside of the facility.

The Audubon Park, adjacent to the Audobon Zoo, provided an excellent base of operation.

roll through the casino parking lot and get a cheeseburger and a bag of chips. Sergeant Major Jensen said, "Little things like that made all the difference in the world."

Portions of the 171st Field Artillery set up shop initially in the convention center after it was evacuated and cleaned the huge facility from top to bottom with hundreds of gallons of bleach. Lieutenant Colonel Paul Metcalfe set a good example and picked up a shovel to begin cleaning piles of debris left behind by evacuees.

Out came the mops and, 12 hours later, it was a sparkling area in which to house soldiers.

The agreement with the City of New Orleans was that troops could occupy the convention center in exchange for providing security for the facility. Command Sergeant Major Tony Riggs said, "It was so big we could drive our largest military vehicle into the hallways. The convention center made great sleeping quarters."

The versatility of the Oklahoma National Guard helped make an unbearable situation "somewhat bearable." Lieutenant Colonel Mike Thompson said, "We had skilled electricians who could flag down a power company truck and help them get power back into a building where we could shelter troops." Thompson's troops found two abandoned freezer trucks on the street and pushed them into their compound to keep food and water cold. "We had to be creative and make living conditions a little better while we did our job." At one time, Thompson's compound was packed with 713 troops, including members of the Puerto Rico National Guard. "And," he said, "we began with only five porta-potties."

One squad from the 1st Battalion, 279th Infantry basically lived on the streets for the first days of their mission until they happened on to a man who was personally standing guard over his fire-engine red Lamborghini on the second floor of a parking garage. When Captain Nate Morgans arrived, the man begged him to provide protection for his car. In exchange, the man gave the National Guard use of his 14-story condominium building.

Morgans claimed the building as company headquarters and moved his soldiers in, two by two, to nice rooms with toilets that flushed. There was running water, but it was contaminated and showers were not usable.

One of the most interesting bases of operation was adjacent to the Audubon Zoo in Audubon Park, a lush 60-acre area along the Mississippi River in Uptown New Orleans. The zoo sustained only minor damage to its buildings and only three animals were killed by Katrina. Troops of

Lieutenant Colonel Monty Brodt's 1st Battalion, 179th Infantry, were patrolling the area when they saw a giraffe's head above a fence.

Hundreds of animals at the zoo had not been evacuated and were cared for by a skeleton staff that sought refuge in the reptile house that was designed to withstand a major hurricane. The building was on high ground and flood waters never touched it. However, the staff was low on food and water when the 179th arrived to help remove large trees in some of the exhibits. The soldiers were invited to set up operations in a large park pavilion.

Lieutenant Colonel Brodt was concerned about field sanitation and the need to dig trenches in the manicured park. However, the park, and the adjacent golf course, were saved from further damage when a stranger walked up and offered to bring porta-potties to the site. A few minutes later, he arrived driving a truck with a trailer full of porta-potties. He had taken them from a construction site where he was employed. Executive Officer Dave Callen made certain the units were tracked so they could be returned to their rightful owner.

Chaplain Norris Burkes' best memory of operating out of the park was conducting a Sunday worship service in a classroom at the Audubon Zoo. To a mixed crowd of zoo employees and guardsmen, he read Psalm 69:1, "Save me, O God, for the waters have come up to my neck. I sink in the miry depths."

Burkes said the Psalm represented the prayer of New Orleans and guardsmen were appointed to answer that prayer. He said, "You are sacred. In the midst of driving through this black water, gagging on fumes from who-knows-what, you are completing a sacred task. You are rescuing the perishing."

Lieutenant Colonel Brodt later moved his soldiers to a compound that once served as an asylum for the mentally ill in New Orleans. It was a six-story building that sustained little damage in the hurricane. At first, it was "crazy hot" because the power was still off. But, Executive Officer Callen, a civil engineer in civilian life, found air conditioning specialists and electricians in other units to bring the power back on. Brodt said, "Within 12 hours, the entire facility was operational and you could hang meat in there. It was the first air conditioning any of us had in weeks. We were ecstatic!"

Charity Hospital in New Orleans 10 days before Katrina hit. Abandoned after Hurricane Katrina, it was guarded by Oklahoma guardsmen.

Soldiers pose in front of one of the giant trees in Audubon Park.

A member of the 1st Battalion, 171st Field Artillery, organizes canned food in a concession stand in the New Orleans Convention Center.

CHAPTER SIX

RESCUE AND RESTORING ORDER

People were walking around in a daze. They were thrilled to see someone new. They cheered to see someone that was going to help.

Lieutenant Colonel Paul Metcalfe

of scenarios—anything we might come across we practice. For our crews, the training paid off."

The 1345th was assigned the task of loading evacuation buses in an orderly manner at the Superdome. It was a dangerous job because the tired, hungry, and thirsty civilians were not in a mood to listen to instructions. But the situation grew smoother. Specialist Heidi Teeter of Clinton admitted that both troops and storm survivors were confused during the first hours,

"Cooperation evolved and the people were glad to see us, having spent so many days in the Superdome with no help in sight."

The 1345th developed a plan to make the bus loading process run more smoothly by setting up five lanes at the end of the mall bridge. Each lane held 50 people who could be loaded onto a bus, then 50 more people would fill the lane. Specialist Teeter observed, "No one ever expressed anger to us. They just wanted to get on the bus."

A terrible spot for suffering was the New Orleans Convention Center where thousands had gone for evacuation even though it was not an official evacuation site. Major Robert Sowards of Arlington, Texas, said the convention center looked like a landfill. He said, "There were no sanitation facilities, and all the basic human functions had to be done outside on the streets. If I hadn't seen it, I would not have believed it." Guardsmen used heavy equipment to begin the cleanup operation around the convention center. Debris was pushed out of the streets, and then the cleanup began inside the center.

For days, Chinook and Black Hawk crews carried soldiers, ammunition, food, and water to designated sites and evacuated survivors from the convention center. Chinook pilot, Captain Clifton Barger of Shawnee, credited crew coordination, communication, training, and a bond among members of the group for the smoothness of their successful mission. Some members of the crew had worked together for nearly 20 years. Barger said, "We practice constantly a diversity

Patients from a flooded nursing home are lifted onto a helicopter for evacuation.

Even though the chaotic situation was somewhat diffused, evacuation from the Superdome was suspended for a time after someone fired shots at a helicopter hovering nearby. Away from the Superdome, lawlessness continued to increase and guardsmen were diverted to keeping the peace.

On the afternoon of September 3, troops from the 1st Battalion, 158th Field Artillery provided relief for the 1345th. By the following day, most of the occupants of the Superdome had been evacuated. Guardsmen had to convince some survivors who wanted to stay that New Orleans was not safe and they had to leave for their own safety.

The Superdome mission ended on September 5. The 1345th had provided aid and help to thousands of people and their presence was a deterrent against horrible crimes that had been committed before guardsmen arrived on the scene. Staff Sergeant Eddy McCain of Oklahoma City said, "The world will remember this event for many years to come. For an Oklahoma Guardsman to be able to say 'I was there and I made a difference in somebody's life' is the greatest feeling."

With order restored in the Superdome, guardsmen turned their attention to other sectors of the city. With National Guard high-water vehicles (HEMTTs), troops conducted search and rescue in deep water. Eleven fuel tankers provided fuel for emergency vehicles. Task Force Red Thunder, made up of Oklahoma Guardsmen and troops from the Army and Air National Guard from Nevada, Rhode Island, Missouri, and Alaska, took responsibility for the convention center evacuation and operated an evacuation side along the Mississippi River.

In addition, troops provided roving guards and worked traffic control in the busiest and most congested areas of the city. Major Sowards and his soldiers provided security in the Ward 5 area, a low-income area where residents verbally admitted they did not trust the New Orleans police but felt the National Guard would care for them.

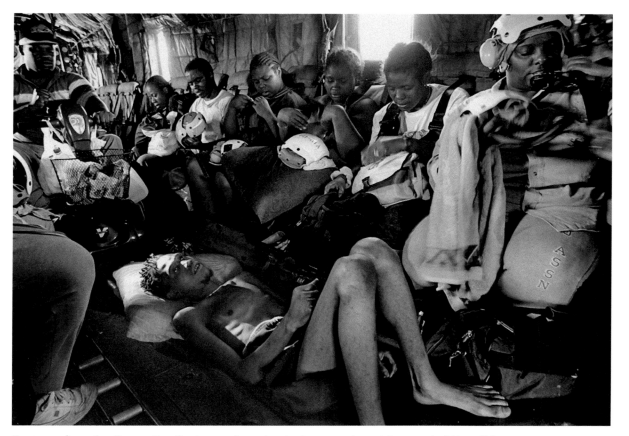

Evacuees from the Convention Center are flown to staging areas to get them out of New Orleans.

Sidewalks were filled with trash outside the New Orleans Convention Center.

Water was a welcome sign for New Orleans residents left behind after Katrina passed through.

National Guardsmen pulled nails and pieces of glass and metal from tires after trucks trudged through debris and water to rescue stranded victims.

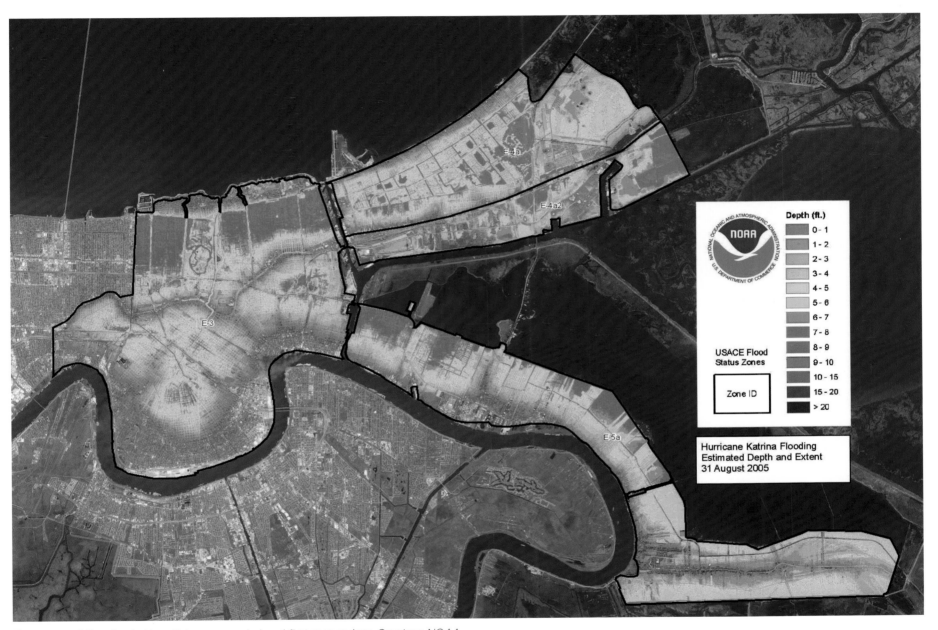

The extent of flooding in New Orleans overwhelmed first responders. *Courtesy NOAA.*

As night approaches, guardsmen head out to protect property.

President Bush arrived to personally view the disaster relief effort. There was still confusion among federal and state leaders as to the line of authority to deal with the tragedy. In *Air Force One*, the President met with Louisiana Governor Blanco and New Orleans Mayor Nagin. There was disagreement as to whether the federal or state government was in control of rescue and relief efforts. Mayor Nagin was abrupt and told the President and Governor that unless they "got on the same page," more lives and property would be lost. The President and Governor went into a private conference and emerged with a solution. The President ordered the military to coordinate efforts with the leadership of Lieutenant General Russel L. Honoré, a native Louisianan.

Honoré was designated commander of Joint Task Force Katrina, responsible for coordinating military relief efforts for Hurricane Katrina-affected areas across the Gulf Coast. Honoré's arrival in New Orleans came after widespread reports of poor performance from local and state officials and FEMA. Honore gained media celebrity and accolades for his gruff management style which contrasted with what many felt were the empty platitudes of civilian officials. In one widely played television clip, Honoré was seen on the streets of the city, barking orders to subordinates and, in one case, berating a soldier who displayed a weapon, telling him "We're on a rescue mission, damn it!"

Mayor Nagin was quoted, "Now, I will tell you this—and I give the President some credit on this—he sent one John Wayne dude down here that can get some stuff done, and his name is Gen. Honoré. And he came off the doggone chopper, and he started cussing and people started moving. And he's getting some stuff done."

General Honoré was the public face of the military effort for news cameras, but history will record that General Deering and his commanders made a huge majority of the day-to-day decisions that controlled the actions of thousands of National Guardsmen and active duty military personnel.

The 700th Support Battalion was a vital part of Katrina rescue operations. On the first day, ten missions were launched to rescue people off roof tops. Commander, Lieutenant Colonel Tonya Chase of Chandler, said 67 people were involved in the missions. "Morale was high,"

Lieutenant General Russel L. Honoré. *Courtesy U.S. Army.*

RULES OF ENGAGEMENT

Oklahoma National Guardsmen were given specific rules of engagement scenarios. Every attempt was made to remain calm and alert and to avoid unholstering or raising a weapon. However, deadly force was authorized by the Rules of Engagement in specific situations, such as a truck driver driving through a gate and nearly hitting the guardsman:

Your life was threatened, and the actions of the driver give you reasonable grounds to suspect he intends to harm others; he used force to gain entry, and the vehicle he is driving is the kind that could contain dangerous cargo. Give the command to halt. If the driver does not stop when ordered, you may use deadly force to stop him.

Major Woody Elmore of Chandler, left, is updated by Sergeant First Class Gary Wayland of Davenport. Both were members of the 1st Battalion, 160th Field Artillery.

Left to right, Specialist Tanner Dupree of Durant, Sergeant Todd Garner of Davis, and Sergeant Jeremy Killman of Yukon, members of the 1345th Transportation Company, load a truck with supplies for fireman in New Orleans.

she said, "the soldiers accomplished each rescue mission in a professional manner."

In addition to rescue operations, the 700th provided Reverse Osmosis Water Purification Units to resupply fire trucks, ambulances, and shower reservoirs. The unit also provided fuel, rations, and class nine parts to supply the mission.

An Oklahoma National Guardsman uses an ATV to coordinate activities along the Mississippi River pier.

Command Sergeant Major Jeffrey Mapes of Alva said, "The fast pace never let up, but the soldiers kept going." At first, the unit supported nearly 17,000 troops. As more supplies arrived, their support base diminished to 5,000 soldiers.

First Lieutenant Roy Banes' A Company linked up with active duty forces and began conducting primary searches with the FBI, U.S. Immigration and Customs Enforcement (ICE) teams, and the New Orleans Police Department. They helped launch boats and used 700th trucks to move through four feet of water to get search teams to the doors of flooded homes. The primary searches were completed during the first seven days of the operation. Personnel from the 700th rescued 76 people and 17 dogs, mostly seeing-eye dogs.

The secondary searches were focused on recovering human remains. However, morale was boosted when a FEMA team using a truck from the 700th forced its way into a flooded home and found an elderly lady still alive in her attic. "It was a long, non-stop schedule that had a positive effect on the long-term experience of the troops," said Commander Chase.

The 700th and other National Guard units followed a specific procedure for the location and removal of dead bodies. A task assigned to Major Tommy Mancino and his intelligence

SAVE THE MONEY

During their deployment in New Orleans, soldiers from the 1345th helped the New Orleans branch of the Federal Reserve Bank retrieve $47 million from a flooded vault.

troops was to track the location of bodies discovered during search and rescue missions. Traditionally, soldiers would have recovered remains and evacuated them immediately. But Katrina was different. FEMA was in charge of the operation to require bodies to be removed by licensed professionals. Guardsmen were allowed to only identify the specific location and report them.

The 45th Infantry Brigade Combat Team tracked the location of bodies on a map at the task force headquarters. A unique part of the identification was to preliminary determine whether a victim had been killed by the flood or by murder. New Orleans had one of the highest murder rates in the country, especially in areas most devastated by flood waters. It was obvious to guardsmen discovering bodies that some were the victims of foul play. Major Mancino said, "When two bullet holes were evident in a man's chest, we knew he had not drowned." Those victims were processed differently and the information relayed to law enforcement officials.

Chaplain Norris Burkes of the 1st Battalion, 179th Infantry, saw things he will never forget. From the backseat of a Humvee, he saw "folks watching us with uncertain eyes, unsure if they should thank us or blame us for not coming sooner."

Chaplain Burkes was confounded by the actions of otherwise law-abiding citizens who succumbed to corruption. He said, "They broke open doors on blocks of stores using stolen cars and even a forklift. People used the storm to finish their quarrels. Criminals settled scores with police officers, and a few bad officers settled scores with whomever they pleased."

The 179th was assigned to a working-class neighborhood with shotgun homes built on elevated stilts. In searching to see if survivors, looters—or worse—dead bodies, were in homes, guardsmen used sledgehammers to gain entry. Sometimes they found all three in the same house.

The 1st Battalion of the 179th rapidly filled the law enforcement vacuum and ended the majority of criminal activity within 48 hours. Lieutenant Colonel Monty Brodt said it was intimidating to criminals that soldiers with M4 carbines were patrolling the streets. Brodt coordinated cordon and search operations with the FBI and Drug Enforcement Agency.

Two hundred forty seven soldiers from the 1st Battalion, 160th Field Artillery brought deep-water rescue capability to flooded areas. Five-ton trucks were used to evacuate survivors and perform both rescue missions and mounted patrols. Often the stranded citizens encountered were elderly and had no way to escape their plight. First Sergeant Darrell Riley of Pauls Valley said, "Our soldiers were compassionate, immediately adopted them, and provided them with daily food and water."

The 145th Cavalry's mission included providing security and helping displaced citizens to move to shelters away from New Orleans. The men and women of the unit went door to door, checking on residents and trying to convince them to leave. Soldiers found stolen property, drugs, alcohol, and weapons. Sometimes the guardsmen were thwarted in their efforts by snarling dogs or confronted with human remains.

Soldiers of the 245th Engineer Battalion were first deployed as a rescue mission. They lengthened the vent tubes on five-ton trucks and drove into the deep water to find people still trapped. After the rescue phase, the unit cleared brush and wrecked cars off streets. The 245th also assisted in cleaning up tree damage at the Audubon Zoo. Sergeant John Barnes of Chouteau and Specialist John Allen of Bixby used a chisel and hammer to carve from a downed oak tree a memorial with the 45th Thunderbird and two Brigade logos. Zoo employees gave the soldiers thunderous applause when the memorial was unveiled.

Even though common sense was that survivors should vacate their flooded homes and be moved to safe locations, it was a difficult job to convince them to do so. Major Mancino said:

We saw large numbers of very poor African American citizens who had not been able to evacuate themselves. They had no cars and no relatives to transport them out of harm's way. They had no money for a bus ticket. They were stuck and did not trust the police, especially the police chief who called the flooded area a war zone and threatened the use of force to remove survivors. We came to provide comfort, food, and water. If people did not want to leave their homes, we continued to check on them to make sure they were okay.

Command Sergeant Major Byron Fry of Owasso said the suffering was great for people left behind:

Oklahoma National Guard soldiers donned masks
to make door-to-door searches for survivors or bodies.

Staff Sergeant Don Davis patrols a flooded neighborhood.

Like something out of a zombie movie, people wandered abandoned roads searching for food and shelter.

Chaplain Norris Burkes

Husband and wife National Guard team, Specialist Eric Burlison of Midwest City, left, and his wife, Specialist Autumn Burlison, assigned to Charlie Company of the 700th Support Battalion.

It was heartbreaking to see someone who had lost almost everything and trying to hold on to what little they had left. They were afraid to leave because their damaged home might be torn down or washed way. They just wanted to protect their last possessions. At that point, we just wanted to make sure they had a roof over their head and enough water and food to make it to a better day.

When Task Force Orleans reached 15,000 troops, the 345th Quartermasters Battalion was mobilized with Commander Lieutenant Colonel Carroll Dobbs of Oklahoma City at the helm. Because General Deering now commanded a division-sized element, it was decided a larger logistics and administration cell was needed. The 345th was normally a water supply battalion, but the need for supporting multiples of the normal number of troops was "a training opportunity," said Dobbs, "that far exceeded anything that could have been implemented at annual training."

First Lieutenant Floyd Roland of Shawnee, a high school teacher in civilian life, was company commander of Charlie Company of the 1st Battalion of the 180th Infantry from the Ada area and was placed in charge of soldiers from Bravo Company from the Poteau and Sallisaw areas. The light infantry troops helped run trucks from the Superdome to the Walmart parking lot. When Roland arrived for duty, he was handed a "visitor's guide to New Orleans," the only maps early-arriving National Guardsmen had to become familiar with the lay of the land.

A problem for mechanics of the 180th was the "crud" in the wheels of the trucks that constantly drove through mud and deep water. "You could hear the crud in the wheels and our mechanics had to repack bearings," said Roland. Maintenance became an important priority for National Guard vehicles in all units because tires were filled with metal and sharp objects, bearings succumbed to mud, and transmissions had to be replaced because of being compromised by mud.

National Guard teams followed a simple method during the recovery phase of the operation. Lieutenant Roland said, "Normally, if there was a smell, we continued the search for bodies and sometimes found only rotting food. But if there was no smell, we stopped." An exception to the rule was in the search of a two-story house that took more than six feet of flood water on the second floor. Even though there was no smell, one of Roland's troops followed a hunch and searched a bedroom where he saw the hand of a woman in her twenties "flop off the side of a bed." She was alive, was removed from the house, and survived at a hospital in a neighboring parish.

One of the companies of the 1st Battalion, 279th Infantry found 40 people trapped in a parking garage. Water stood on the first floor, so there was no way out. Troops drove five-ton trucks through the deep water and were met by a cheering crowd. They had been shot at by gang members and harassed by a band of thugs before being rescued by guardsmen.

Troops were always on the lookout for looters.

Wolf said, "It wasn't hard to figure out. If you saw someone rolling a flat screen down the street and follow them to their apartment where there were ten other TVs, it was pretty obvious." In such situations, the looters were turned over to law enforcement who established a makeshift detention center at the Greyhound bus station." Confiscated stolen items were stored in one of the freezers at the Culinary Institute until they could be turned over to police.

A sad rescue took place less than two blocks from Lieutenant Colonel Mike Thompson's headquarters. His troops discovered a 600-pound woman who had been pulled from the flood waters and left with only two gallons of water and a small amount of food on the top of a crate in a parking garage. Personnel from Bravo Company of the 1st Battalion, 279th Infantry, saved the woman's life. They commandeered a forklift, put the crate and the woman in the back of a pickup truck, and delivered her to an evacuation point.

As the flood waters began receding, Command Sergeant Byron Fry's battalion was known as "dog killers." Most units had to reluctantly put down dogs left behind by evacuees because they roamed in packs and tried to consume dead human bodies. Fry said, "They were starving and ferocious and tried to attack soldiers." Fry and his troops were all dog lovers, but killed 15 dogs. "There was no choice," he said.

Major General Harry Wyatt, III, adjuntant general for Oklahoma, visits with children evacuated to Camp Gruber.

CHAPTER SEVEN

SAFE AND SECURE AT CAMP GRUBER

For once they could lay down and sleep and not worry about being killed. Some told me they were never leaving Gruber. They were comfortable, felt safe, and were secure.

Lieutenant Colonel Ronald Ragland

F ive days after Hurricane Katrina devastated New Orleans and the Gulf Coast, the Houston Astrodome and dozens of centers throughout Texas and northern Louisiana were running over with people. Oklahoma was again asked to help. General Wyatt offered Camp Gruber, near Braggs, Oklahoma, as a secure haven for busloads of storm victims desperately trying to escape the chaos in their cities. In addition to experiencing anxiety from Katrina, the federal government was confused about where to take evacuees, forcing some people to be confined to buses for up to 72 hours.

A guard tower at Camp Gruber stood over a secure compound which held German prisoners-of-war during World War II. *Courtesy Oklahoma Historical Society.*

An Army band at Camp Gruber with barracks in the background. *Courtesy Oklahoma Historical Society.*

The Post Exchange at Camp Gruber in 1944. *Courtesy Oklahoma Historical Society.*

Within 24 hours, 265 members of the Oklahoma Army and Air National Guard, permanent personnel at Camp Gruber, and five Naval reservists who had not been sent to New Orleans and the Gulf Coast were activated for what headquarters called "Operation Sooner." Soldiers received urgent orders to report to Gruber because the first busloads of evacuees of the storm were expected to arrive soon. There was little time to prepare for them.

Camp Gruber had a long military history. In 1942, after America's entry into World War II, the United States Army Corps of Engineers began building a troop training facility for 35,000 troops. The federal government controlled more than 30,000 acres near the town of Braggs, in Muskogee County. The training center was named for Brigadier General Edmund L. Gruber, a longtime artillery officer at Fort Sill, Oklahoma.

Manhattan-Long Construction Company was the winning bidder and built 1,731 frame buildings, including hospitals, barracks, administration buildings, a bakery, chapels, a laundry, mess halls, a gymnasium, repair shops, guard houses, motor repair shops, and even a theater. Utilities were added and State Highway 10 was relocated around the base. An old ranch house complex served as the post commander's billet.

Within a few months, soldiers arrived at Camp Gruber for training in infantry, field artillery, and tank destruction on thousands of acres of firing ranges, bayonet courts, grenade courts, and obstacles courses which resembled the roads, fields, and hedgerows soldiers would see in Europe. More than 44,000 troops either served or were trained at Camp Gruber which also employed 4,000 civilian workers.

Camp Gruber was deactivated in 1947 after the war ended. By the 1960s, most of the camp's original buildings were removed or destroyed. In 1967, the Oklahoma Military Department leased approximately 23,000 acres from the federal government to establish Gruber as a state-operated training area. Another 10,000 acres were added to bring the size of the camp to 87 square miles. New buildings were constructed for summer field exercises and weekend training of National Guardsmen.

On September 2, 2005, guardsmen such as Colonel Doug Haught of Elk City was notified to report immediately. Haught, who served as a state court judge in Beckham County, was told he should arrive at Gruber by nightfall because buses may start arriving at any time. Haught was the base commander during the operation.

Soldiers of the 120th Engineer Battalion in Okmulgee, the 138th Security Forces Squadron in Tulsa, and the 137th Security Forces Squadron in Oklahoma City were activated to primarily provide security for the expected influx for as many as 2,500 victims who were making a 26-hour bus ride from New Orleans. The victims were officially identified as "displaced civilians" for purposes of reporting and communication.

Within a short time, National Guard troops and hundreds of representatives from other local, state, and federal agencies and relief organizations were ready to receive, secure, and provide housing, food, and water for the evacuees. The Red Cross, Oklahoma Highway Patrol (OHP), FBI, State Emergency Management Services, FEMA, State Department of Health, Salvation Army, Goodwill, and the Muskogee Fire Department provided more than 500 people to work alongside the 265 military personnel.

Half the military contingent came from the 120th and 55 troops were permanent staff at Camp Gruber. Sergeant First Class Ron Mordecai of Edmond was the First Sergeant of Charlie Company of the 120th and reported to the Okemah armory to ready his troops for a bus ride to Camp Gruber. There was only time to issue weapons and provide limited information. The mission was moving so quickly, Mordecai said, "A lot of the briefings were given on the bus. We really didn't know what to expect, but we made plans to set up a perimeter to secure the area set aside for the evacuees."

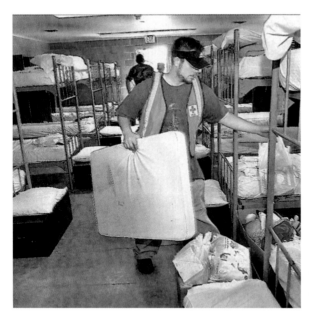

Red Cross workers prepare beds for Hurricane Katrina evacuees.

The 120th set up shop in one of the old barracks buildings. Commanders went over rules of engagement. But, the following day, weapons were taken from the guardsmen. Sergeant Mordecai said, "It was a strange feeling. We had just gotten back from Iraq and were accustomed to having our weapons." Officials in charge believed that members of the Air Guard units and local, state, and federal law enforcement officers with guns would provide enough manpower.

The Red Cross was the lead civilian agency of the Camp Gruber mission. However, Red Cross personnel were overwhelmed with the number of evacuees on their way and the security concerns. To make certain that personnel and evacuees were safe, Oklahoma Governor Henry placed the Oklahoma Highway Patrol in control of the operation. The Muskogee, Tulsa, and Oklahoma County Sheriff's Departments also sent task force teams to help with any trouble. The OHP quickly dispatched units to Dallas, Texas, as the buses were passing through. OHP then notified military officials when the buses might arrive.

A United States marshal also was assigned at Camp Gruber. There was legal issue of what law enforcement agency was in charge. The land was owned by the federal government, but leased by the Oklahoma Military Department. The issue was never resolved but did not present a problem. All National Guardsmen and law enforcement officers worked as a team.

The first bus arrived from New Orleans at 3:00 a.m. on September 3. Lieutenant Colonel Ronald Ragland of Vian, the fulltime facility manager and deputy commander at Gruber, remembered, "It was sad to see these hopeless people get off the bus with hardly anything. Most of them carried only a Walmart sack of their personal belongings." The buses had been traveling in limbo after being turned away at shelters in Dallas, told to go back to Houston, then sent to Camp Gruber. The latrines on the buses were overflowing.

The evacuees had not been told where they were going. The next morning at daylight, they asked guardsmen, "Where are we? Is this Houston? Is this Dallas?" They were informed they were in the middle of eastern Oklahoma, a long way from a big city.

Guardsmen worked with volunteers from relief agencies to check identification and make certain that arriving evacuees did not have weapons. One lady walked up to a National Guardsman and revealed she had a pistol. She was a police officer in New Orleans who had left and kept her weapon for personal security during the long bus ride. She gave up her weapon.

Michael Overall, a reporter for the *Tulsa World*, chronicled the arrival of the evacuees at Gruber:

Volunteers gagged from the stench when they climbed on board the buses where some passengers weren't moving. Some were slumped over, eyes closed or staring blankly, and did not respond to questions. A frantic, and thankfully false report went out on official walkie-talkies, "We have bodies on board." Not dead bodies, as officials first thought, but bodies too tired and, in some cases, too dehydrated to move.

Camp Gruber was ready for the tired and frightened people. Sheets and blankets were on beds in barracks. The open-bay barracks housed about 40 bunks, or sometimes double that number if stacked. Commanders tried to make the processing as easy and quick as possible. Lieutenant Colonel Ragland said, "We understood they were frustrated and probably needed to sleep for three or four days. Everybody's attitude in our force was to bring them in here and make them feel comfortable." There was a male barracks, a female barracks, and a separate facility where families could stay together.

Guardsmen and law enforcement officers kept a close eye on the evacuees. Information from New Orleans suggested that drug dealers and gang members were among the evacuees. In fact, a drug deal went down just outside the Camp Gruber gates and suspects were arrested by officers from the Braggs Police Department. Lieutenant Colonel Ragland said, "We used National Guard personnel to observe. We identified troublemakers and sent them on their way. It was not a secret to the people that we were watching 24/7."

When officials learned that some of the evacuees were trying to take over the barracks and charge other evacuees for preferential areas to sleep, guardsmen identified them and expelled them from the base and took them to Tulsa with enough money for a bus ticket out of Oklahoma. A National Guard soldier was assigned to each floor of the barracks to keep theft down and prevent fights or any other mischief.

Other buses began arriving at 30-minute intervals. A total of 39 buses eventually brought 1,592 evacuees to Gruber. The evacuees were housed in eight two-story barracks and a single one-story building. The non-air-conditioned buildings were quickly made comfortable with the installation of 60-ton units. Personnel worked around the clock to install the units. The base medical building was occupied by state emergency medical teams. The Southern Baptist Disaster Relief Ministry set up two dining facilities and served three hot meals a day. Even a temporary post office was set up for people to receive mail.

The detailed processing of the evacuees was a great help for Red Cross volunteers to notify families that their missing loved ones were at Gruber. The efficiency of the database and the close cooperation between Camp Gruber and other agencies worked well. Within a day of the first arrival, families came to pick up missing family members. Guardsmen had a good feeling when they were able to escort someone to the front gate to be reunited with family.

In addition to reuniting families, there were other success stories. Two families paid utility deposits on homes in Muskogee and another man was hired as a cook at Connors State College in Warner and found a house to rent.

Gruber officials had no problem with allowing anyone to leave, but they wanted every departure documented. Buses were dispatched to the Tulsa airport and the Muskogee bus station for evacuees to leave Oklahoma.

There were more than 30 children at Gruber with no parents. Some were only five and six years old. Officials received a call from Mississippi from a frantic father looking for his

A priest visits with hurricane evacuees at Camp Gruber.

A birthday party for evacuees.

The displaced were allowed to move freely only in a designated area of Camp Gruber, between Third Street and Sixth Street, and Central Europe Street and Southern France Street. It was the main mission of the 120th Engineers to secure the perimeter. Tight security included OHP troopers and sheriffs' deputies driving the perimeter. Sergeant Mordecai said, "There was so much law enforcement there, there couldn't have been more than 25 to 30 feet between vehicles."

After a while, evacuees were allowed to visit nearby towns. The Red Cross issued every person an identification card. They were allowed to leave, but needed the card to get back on base.

Officials tried to make living at Gruber as "normal" as possible. A television with satellite reception was set up in every building. Walmart donated the televisions and the satellite service were gifts from DIRECTV and DISH Network. A band volunteered to play music for two hours every night after dinner. The sounds of New Orleans jazz drifted into the Oklahoma night air.

Twenty-four hours after most of the evacuees had arrived at Gruber, they were "finding a sense of peace." Personnel Officer, Captain Brian Deshazo of Ft. Gibson, observed, "Some were eating their lunch on the grassy commons while others walked quietly down the streets of the fledgling community, enjoying the feeling of space after days of crowded conditions in the Superdome." Nearby, the sounds of boys playing football created a neighborhood atmosphere.

Company C electrician sergeant, Tom Mitchell of Okmulgee, said much of the duty

eight-year-old son. One mother who was missing two of her teenage children explained, "They just threw us on buses at the Superdome and told us the buses were all going to the same place. Then, they didn't." Some buses went to Texas, others went to Arkansas and Mississippi.

The National Guard asked the Oklahoma Department of Human Services to assume control of the children and reunite them with their parents or guardians. There was also assistance from the National Center for Missing and Exploited Children. Within a few days, each parentless child at Gruber was reunited with parents or guardians.

involved "simply being there" for the people who had endured chaos. He said, "We were a little apprehensive when the first bus arrived, but we knew how much these people were hurting and we wanted to help them." Mitchell said the key to the success of the mission was to show respect to the people, "We believed we needed to treat them as we would want to be treated and get them settled and comfortable as quickly as possible."

Volunteers from churches came by the hundreds to provide counseling services during the week and church services on the weekend. Churches also brought literally hundreds of boxes of clothing for the evacuees who had only the clothing they left their homes with. Soon donations of shoes and clothing were "stacked to the ceiling," and every evacuee was adequately clothed and the children had toys, roller blades, and bicycles.

Communication was important. Lieutenant Colonel Ragland had a computer bank set up for people to use the internet. Forty phones were made available for evacuees. The OHP held an informational session every night for people who wanted to attend. Inside each barracks, evacuees elected a spokesman to ask questions. Ragland said, "We tried to be very open about the situation and keep everyone as informed as best as we could." At night, OHP troopers stood in a circle and answered every question. If people were shy, they held back after the meeting and talked one-on-one with troopers.

The tight security "weeded out" the "bad apples" that remained. A man who overdosed on Methadone was taken to jail. A volunteer who was getting "too friendly with a child" was escorted from the base. A known sex offender was identified and taken to Tulsa for him to rent a car and leave the state. One night, a drunk driver was apprehended at Building 108. He was the owner of a local bar who had been providing rides to and from his business. He was detained and a sober driver came to pick him up.

Early one morning, Lieutenant Colonel Ragland came across an elderly lady sitting outside her barracks. She could not sleep because she could not make contact with her grandson who was in the Marine Corps and stationed on the East Coast. Ragland contacted the Red Cross who tracked down the Marine so that he could have a conference call with his grandmother and know that she was alive and well.

Even though most evacuees were doing well, illness struck others. A kidney transplant patient was taken to a hospital because he had not received his anti-rejection medicine. Many people complained of swollen feet. More than 50 evacuees were taken to hospitals for treatment and more than 200 were treated in the first week for minor ailments and injuries at the base clinic. A 58-year-old woman was taken from an arriving bus to a nearby hospital where she died.

Camp Gruber Command Sergeant Major Bill SanMillan of Stuart was placed in charge of setting up school for the children. He was the superintendent of schools in Stroud, Oklahoma. Buses from Tahlequah Public Schools arrived at Gruber each morning to pick up children for

The evacuees I have talked to at Camp Gruber say they have been treated better in Oklahoma than anywhere else. I commend all Oklahomans who worked so hard to help others in need.

Governor Brad Henry

classes and even ran buses in the evening to take students back to Tahlequah for school events.

When the federal government began issuing checks to evacuees, a Muskogee bank established a small office in which checks could be cashed. Some of the people began to use their money to buy food and do their own Cajun cooking. National Guardsmen were often invited for a meal with the evacuees. Lieutenant Colonel Ragland observed, "The effort that we were putting forward and how we got treated back from them made it very rewarding."

The work of the 120th was praised by Brigadier General Gary D. Bray of Tulsa, deputy commander of the Oklahoma Army Guard. He said, "For some time, this has been the 'go to' battalion in the state. We knew when this mission came up, we could count on them."

Governor Henry and First Lady Kim Henry visited Camp Gruber during the second week of the operation. The Governor said the professionalism of the Oklahoma National Guard was without equal and that Operation Sooner would continue until the last evacuee was taken care of.

For the children, the First Lady brought huge boxes of toys donated by Oklahomans attending Septembfest, an annual celebration at the Governor's Mansion. She also toured a Head Start program set up at Gruber by the Oklahoma Partnership for School Readiness.

Cash payments and housing vouchers from FEMA allowed evacuees at Camp Gruber to leave faster than initially expected. Help from the Red Cross and other charitable organizations and churches also expedited the exodus. After five weeks, only 28 evacuees remained and Governor Henry ordered the operation to close on October 6, after operating for 34 days. The final 28 people were moved to hotels in Tulsa and Muskogee.

The Katrina relief effort at Camp Gruber cost more than $5 million. Staff Sergeant Lavonda Cathey of Chandler, the post budget analyst, managed the expenditures and made certain the right officials received reimbursement requests for individual soldiers, the National Guard, and other state agencies. The OHP was reimbursed $753,097, much of it in overtime pay for troopers who provided security. The Oklahoma National Guard received more than $400,000, a partial reimbursement for calling up guardsmen to staff Gruber while the evacuees were there. Camp Gruber was reimbursed more than $200,000 just to replace blankets and mattresses. The State Health Department, in charge of the base medical clinic, received $329,000.

As the operation wound down and National Guardsmen went home, there was a great sense of accomplishment. Governor Henry said, "Members of our Army and Air Guard have stepped up to the plate in an incredible way." Sergeant Lavonda Cathey said, "I will never forget all the people of our unit coming together to take care of people in need. The communities just came out and took care of everybody."

First Lady Kim Henry distributes toys to children of evacuees at Camp Gruber.

roops from the 1st Battalion, 171st Field Artillery guard a water pumping station in New Orleans.

CHAPTER EIGHT

UNFORGETTABLE STORIES

We were infantrymen with rifles, but we weren't there to shoot people. We were there to give somebody a ride, some water, or help them, because that's what the people on the street needed.

Captain Gerald Mastin

Army Chaplain Lieutenant Colonel Jack Byas conducts a chapel service for members of 1st Battalion, 160th Field Artillery.

Not every person the National Guard encountered in New Orleans was looking for help. Some intended to take advantage of the disaster for personal gain by looting stores and residences, destroying the property of others, or hurting or killing fellow residents. On occasion, ruffians threw bricks at guardsmen, then ran into houses where troops had to kick in the door to detain them. Some people settled old scores by murdering enemies.

Sergeant James McIntire of Skiatook and other members of Charlie Company of the 1st Battalion, 279th Infantry, knew that their mission would be hard from the moment they donned body armor and were issued weapons and ammunition. Once on the ground, after circling a busy airport in a hot C-130 cargo aircraft for 90 minutes, McIntire and his fellow soldiers began ridding the flooded areas of "the criminal element." People were breaking into neighbors' abandoned houses, setting buildings and cars on fire, and harassing others who were not able to evacuate.

"As soon as we showed up," McIntire said, "they usually started running." A few tried to resist. McIntire said, "We let it be known that we weren't going to mess around with any of that." Charlie Company had to run off intruders to a World War II museum that was trashed for no reason at all. Medals of past heroes were just thrown around and the intruders defecated on chairs and the floor.

We weren't there
to sight see; we
weren't tourists,
we were soldiers
and we stayed
focused until
we were done.

Brigadier General Myles L. Deering

Members of Company B, 1st Battalion, 279th Infantry on foot patrol in the French Quarter of New Orleans.

A soldier from the 160th Field Artillery manning a checkpoint to limit traffic into flooded areas.

McIntire and his squad came across a young woman being raped. The soldiers stopped the attack, only to have the woman get mad and claim her attackers were her "ticket out of town." Other duty for Charlie Company was just as unpleasant, but in a different way. When McIntire and other soldiers guarded Charity Hospital, they were responsible for clearing the 19-floor, three-wing hospital of rats with a single pellet gun and helping clean out the morgue. At least after the stay in the hospital, the unit was moved to the Hyatt House Hotel.

McIntire, only 24 years old, but 6'7" with a muscular build and a civilian job as a jailer at the Tulsa County jail, often had to intervene when smaller squad members tried to take down a suspect obviously under the influence of drugs. The squad arrested a New Orleans police officer who was pushing a stolen television down the street on wheels, even though it had a water line through the center of the screen.

Charlie Company and about two dozen other members of the Oklahoma National Guard came down with a virus that caused them to break out in a bumpy, red rash, sometimes from head to foot. When the first four soldiers came down with the rash, they were hospitalized overnight as a precaution on the USS *Iwo Jima*. When it was determined that the rash was all too common in the Deep South, the soldiers were returned to duty with medicine to ease their symptoms. Other guardsmen developed thrush, diagnosed by large lumps on the tongue. Medical personnel took care of that problem with penicillin or amoxicillin shots.

Toward the end of the mission, one squad leader wanted his men to be able to say they had seen famous Bourbon Street. When the troops were stopped by a member of the 82nd Airborne, the squad leader said, "You better step the hell out of my way because my men are walking down Bourbon Street before we leave this town."

Oklahoma guardsmen frequently had an opportunity to make a difference in someone's life, one-on-one. An example was the encounter of Staff Sergeant Eric Wolf with a man whose home was destroyed, had walked miles from a checkpoint to check on his property, and his cell phone was dead with no way to contact his family. Even though Wolf was ending his shift for the night, he took the man back to his home, reconnected him to his vehicle, and recharged his phone so he could call his daughter to let her know he was alive. Wolf said, "When I looked into his eyes, I saw hope and relief. I believe it was a unique opportunity that God gave me to make a difference in one guy's life."

During the recovery phase as the water receded, First Lieutenant Floyd Roland and his unit were treated to Cajun food and soft drinks by both returning police officers and residents. As the New Orleans Police Department had officers return to duty, check points in certain parts of the city were handed over to them. Roland said, "When they showed up, they had ice chests full of beverages."

Roland's troops patrolled a large cemetery for vandals. For three nights they saw a man sneak into the cemetery that was unlike any Oklahoma cemetery he had ever seen. Roland said, "Among

A National Guard helicopter drops sandbags to strengthen a New Orleans levee.

Members of the 279th Infantry Battalion ready for the next phase of their mission in New Orleans.

those huge statues and burial chambers we found the man camping out. He had been pilfering what he needed and was living in the middle of the cemetery trying to ride this thing out."

Staff Sergeant Jerome Umphrey of Norman, Alpha Company, 1st Battalion, 179th Infantry, led a squad that initially tried to convince residents to leave their flooded or destroyed homes. Umphrey is a native of Louisiana and "could roll in and start talking Cajun to them." The instant rapport gave Umphrey a leg up on others in the same situation. He said, "I convinced many of them to get on our trucks so we could take them to a staging area to ride a bus out of this place."

Umphrey's company stayed on the manicured lawn of an Episcopal Church Rectory built in the 19th century. The Rectory still had power and guardsmen "threw extension cords over the wall so phones could be charged and other electronic devices could be powered." In the Rectory garage, troops found four camping solar showers. With some Oklahoma ingenuity, along with PVC pipe and ponchos, showers were created. Five-gallon buckets of water provided sufficient water. There was no need to heat the water because of the hot and sultry weather.

The Rectory caretaker allowed soldiers to play pool on the second floor. From that vantage point someone noticed an older man with dreadlocks and a stocking cap wreck his bicycle in the middle of the street. When a medic reached the man he was unresponsive, but had $900 of new money in his wallet. The man's name was Fred and he had just cashed his check from the Veterans Administration. Sergeant Umphrey said, "We loaded the veteran in an ambulance but took his bicycle back to the Rectory so the man could retrieve it later." During the recovery, an Associated Press photographer took a photograph of the incident. The photo later appeared in newspapers across the nation, including back home in *The Oklahoman*.

The responsibility of Brigade Chaplain, Lieutenant Colonel Michael Taylor of Bethel Acres, was to make sense out of the suffering and death seen by his fellow guardsmen. If a soldier became bored with long shifts keeping people from coming back into devastated areas and asked, "Why are we still here?" Chaplain Taylor tried to explain that a shotgun house might not be much, but it still belonged to somebody and that whatever is left in that house deserved to have guardsmen protect it, regardless of value. Taylor frequently told soldiers, "It might be monotonous and tiring, but what we are doing is still very important to the people who could not be here to protect their own stuff."

The sight and smell of dead bodies was traumatic for many soldiers. One young guardsman saw a body floating and tied it to a fence so it could be collected at a later time. That night, the soldier was bothered and wanted to talk about it with the chaplain. Taylor asked him, "Did you treat the body with the same respect like you would want your father or grandfather treated?" When the soldier said, "Yes," Chaplain Taylor assured

A soldier from Company B, 279th Infantry, convinces a resident to leave her damaged home to be evacuated to safety.

him that it was the only course of action that he could take. Taylor counseled many guardsmen who were horrified to see a dead body for the first time in their lives.

A heartwarming story in the aftermath of Katrina began when Headquarters Battery First Sergeant Michael Haws of Carrier helped an elderly lady, Lillian Galloway, and her husband load onto separate buses after their house was destroyed by the hurricane. After the buses left, Haws noticed a purple bag on the ground that contained money and

personal documents. It was all the savings the Galloways had.

Unsure of what to do with the bag, Haws made a list of its contents and handed it over to Chaplain Taylor who established a chain of custody and accountability and asked Intelligence Officer First Lieutenant Teri Scroggins of El Reno to place the bag in the unit safe.

Galloway's husband died on the bus before it arrived in Houston, Texas. Mrs. Galloway realized she had lost their savings and began

TRUST AND RESPECT

Even when the people did not trust their own police, they trusted the Oklahoma National Guard. The people said our soldiers were respectful and treated them with dignity regardless of how cold, wet, hungry, and naked they were.

Major General Harry "Bud" Wyatt, III.

Governor Brad Henry addresses the memorial service for Katrina victims and thanked the Oklahoma National Guard for their service.

to pray for its recovery. She called it "an absolute miracle" when she was notified by a family support coordinator in Houston that the 45th Field Artillery had her bag secured. Sergeant Haws and Chaplain Taylor were flown to Houston to return the bag to Mrs. Galloway. As television cameras captured the moment, Mrs. Galloway called the Oklahoma Guardsmen involved in returning her savings "her angels."

Chaplain Taylor had a personal opportunity to save the life of a man in his mid-seventies who was stranded on the streets unable to attend kidney dialysis needed to keep him alive. All Taylor knew the man by was "Bubba." At first, Taylor could not take Bubba with him because he did not know the location of the nearest medical evacuation staging area. But the chaplain told Bubba, who claimed to be a preacher, he would come back.

Taylor found the medical evacuation point a quarter mile away and, with the help of others who found an abandoned luggage rack, pushed Bubba to the evacuation point. Along the route

The 145th Army Band of the Oklahoma Army National Guard provided music for the ceremony honoring victims and survivors of Hurricane Katrina.

Bubba shouted, "Hallelujah, praise the Lord, thank you Jesus." Bubba believed he would be delivered, and he was. Crews loaded him onto the next helicopter leaving the hurricane-stricken area around the Superdome.

First Lieutenant Chris Isch of Edmond, a land surveyor and civil engineer in civilian life, was the platoon leader of Alpha Battery of the 1st Battalion, 160th Field Artillery based in Pauls Valley. Isch's platoon spent much of their time on the ground in "presence patrols." The purpose of the patrol was to act as a deterrent to any type of criminal activity and to reassure anyone who stayed in their homes that the National Guard was on duty to protect them and their property. Isch saw many residents who stayed behind. If their first floor was flooded, they lived on the second floor. One family lived in a tent in their yard because their house was uninhabitable. Isch and his troops always stopped and made certain survivors had plenty of water and rations.

IN FAITH AND HOPE
WE LIFT OUR EYES
FOR THOSE AT REST
AND THOSE WHO RISE

PRESENTED BY THE OKLAHOMA
NATIONAL GUARD ON BEHALF OF
THE PEOPLE OF OKLAHOMA

WE DEDICATE THIS TREE IN
COMMEMORATION OF THE SURVIVORS
AND THOSE LOST TO THE RAVAGES OF
HURRICANE KATRINA
SEPTEMBER 30 2005

THIS GRANITE SLAB WAS RECOVERED FROM THE
RUINS OF THE OKLAHOMA CITY
ALFRED P. MURRAH FEDERAL BUILDING
DESTROYED APRIL 19, 1995

A memorial cut from stone from the Alfred P. Murrah Federal Building in Oklahoma City accompanied the planting of an Oklahoma Redbud tree in New Orleans.

To Isch, the biggest challenge for the Guard was dealing with people who could not be convinced to leave. He said:

> They didn't want to be evacuated. They didn't want to be told what to do. It was their house. It was their land and trying to convince them it was in their best interest to leave often fell on deaf ears. They did not want to hear it.

Nothing was routine for Isch and his soldiers. Operating from bases of operation that ranged from the Audubon Zoo, Louis Armstrong Park, and the Fair Grounds Racetrack Course, troops of the 160th ran into a strange situation one night. Isch received an urgent call from one of his squad leaders of "a sticky situation." When Isch arrived, squad members huddled behind their vehicle because an obviously-intoxicated man stood in the street holding a pistol. Isch called for backup from New Jersey state troopers. After 30 minutes, the man dropped the gun. He was a doctor who had "hit his breaking point" after processing dead bodies day after day.

The calm approach to the otherwise dangerous situation was a tribute to the Oklahoma soldiers' discipline and training. Isch said, "The NCOs did an excellent job of keeping the junior enlisted guys without a lot of experience in check and helped them maintain their bearing."

Humanitarian missions of the Oklahoma National Guard during September, 2005, frequently involved people who were devastated at having to leave their pets. Five years after Katrina, Susan Young of New Orleans wrote

General Deering and thanked him for members of the 45th Brigade driving her to her flooded home to rescue her dog, Hershey, and cat, Clio. Young wrote, "Hershey passed away two years ago of old age, not of starvation and dehydration had it not been for the Oklahoma National Guard."

By the middle of September, there was a sense of "things being under control" and the National Guard working itself out of a job. Citizens were allowed to return to areas in which floodwaters had receded. But then, Hurricane Rita confounded the best-laid plans.

Rita was the fourth-most intense Atlantic hurricane ever recorded. On September 21, Rita reached peak winds of 180 miles-per-hour. In New Orleans, General Deering ordered troops under his command to move to high ground and moved non-essential personnel out of the path of the storm. Rita weakened in the Gulf of Mexico, missed New Orleans, and targeted Texas where 113 deaths were reported. Rita did more than $12 billion dollars in damage to Louisiana and Texas.

As Rita roared past southern Louisiana, heavy rain poured on previously breached canals in New Orleans. Officials feared dried-out areas would flood again. To help the situation, Chinook helicopters from Detachment 1, Company G, 149th Aviation Battalion of the Oklahoma Army National Guard assisted in dropping hundreds of sandbags weighing up to 10,000 pounds each onto the levees to stem the flow of water.

On September 30, a Task Force Orleans memorial ceremony was held at Holy Name

Louisiana Governor Kathleen Blanco praised the service of the Oklahoma National Guard.

of Jesus Church on the campus of Loyola University of New Orleans. Its purpose was to honor those who were lost in the disaster and celebrate the storm's survivors. Louisiana Governor Kathleen Blanco joined Oklahoma Governor Brad Henry and First Lady Kim Henry in praising the 2,300 Oklahoma National Guardsmen who were credited with saving more than 2,500 lives as they patrolled the streets with state and federal response forces. Nearly 500 of the rescues were accomplished by Oklahoma Army Guard helicopters in the early days of the operation.

The women of the Oklahoma National Guard served proudly in the Katrina mission.

General Deering reflected on the successful mission of his citizen soldiers who left their families and jobs to "professionally" and "efficiently" bring New Orleans back from the brink of total destruction. As part of the ceremony, a Redbud Tree from Oklahoma was planted and a Memorial Stone paying tribute to the efforts of the Oklahoma National Guard was dedicated.

New Orleans was better when Oklahoma Guardsmen received word on October 3, 2005, that orders were given to return to Oklahoma. Traffic lights were working, the putrid smell was mostly gone, and people were returning to the streets. The smell and toxic residue had been cleaned up partially because of the heavy rain produced by Hurricane Rita. Much of the waste washed into storm sewers.

The once tempo of "fast and furious" of the first two weeks of the mission calmed to a "busy, but steady pace," according to Colonel Pat Scully of Choctaw, who had spent weeks managing relations with media personnel as the official spokesman for the brigade.

Knowing they were headed home, Oklahoma troops took a day to pack their gear and clean the filth from their vehicles. Some guardsmen did not intend to leave New Orleans alone. In the truck of Sergeant First Class Robert Apala of Hartshorne was a furry, four-legged evacuee named Sarge. The dog had been rescued from an apartment in New Orleans and stayed with Apala's unit. It was impossible to locate Sarge's owner, so Apala took the dog to his country home.

To make certain that Oklahoma soldiers returned to Oklahoma in a healthy condition, guardsmen directed their convoys through Camp Maxey outside Paris, Texas. Meals were ready for the troops, blood was drawn, mechanics checked out vehicles that had seen extraordinary duty in floodwaters and toxic waste. Soldiers were asked if they had any ailments, even minor conditions. Everything was documented. "It was an intelligent decision to have us stop in unison at Maxey," reflected Sergeant Major Steven Jensen, "If we had waited until everyone returned to their home armories, they would have gone in four directions and we would never be properly debriefed."

CHAPTER NINE

REFLECTIONS

When we left, I knew we had made a huge difference in the lives of thousands of people. People were no longer living in fear, peeking out between curtains because of pillaging gangs. When they saw us, they were able to come out into the sunshine. Many were sad to see the Thunderbird leave.

Lieutenant Colonel Mike Thompson

Major events are an aggregate of individual experiences. The story of the Oklahoma National Guard's response to the nation's worst natural disaster is not about the ferocity of the storm, the unbridled destruction of wind and water, or the inability of government to secure the safety of its people.

Instead, the story of the Oklahoma National Guard's response to Hurricane Katrina is about the individual experiences of more than 2,300 Oklahoma men and women who willingly sacrificed to save and restore the lives of people they had never met and probably never will.

People see themselves in mirrors through reflections. Years after serving in the most significant humanitarian mission of our generation, many National Guardsmen reflected on the goodness of their actions and lessons learned from making split-second decisions when life and limb depended upon it.

These thoughtful reflections, looking back at the muck, mire, death, and destruction of Hurricane Katrina—and more importantly, how Oklahomans responded to it—are recorded with the military rank of officers and enlisted men and women at the time of the 2005 mission to the Big Easy.

MAJOR GENERAL HARRY M. "BUD" WYATT, III
KETCHUM

Helping our neighbors in Louisiana is the very reason we joined the National Guard. What a great experience we had by knowing we did a good job and should feel good about our effort. What we learned has paid great dividends. Through refining command and control and the increased use of technology, the Oklahoma National Guard is more efficient and ready-for-action than ever before. If we had another Katrina, we could handle it, and we probably could do it with fewer soldiers and less resources and still provide a superb response.

BRIGADIER GENERAL MYLES DEERING
NORMAN

Katrina gave me a better understanding of what it means to be a citizen soldier. I understood more clearly how willing our soldiers were to pitch in to help their neighbors. Of our troops on the ground, more than 30 were up for reenlistment during the weeks on duty in New Orleans. Each of the men and women reenlisted. That speaks volumes to the value they saw in not only serving the nation in times of crisis and war, but also in serving our sister states.

I am so proud of the soldiers and airmen who gladly reported for duty in the worst of sanitary conditions. Because of their actions, we did nothing but bring good will to Oklahoma. Many soldiers told me their duty in New Orleans was harder than duty in Iraq. Yes, it was hard. But as the years pass, we think more of the good times than the bad times. We think more of the service we provided than the inconvenience of no showers and rashes and living in a constant state of sweat. I never had a soldier tell me that what we did was not a thing of value for all time.

LIEUTENANT GENERAL H. STEVEN BLUM
CHIEF OF THE NATIONAL GUARD BUREAU
2003-2008

At the darkest moment, America's National Guard arrived to pull order from chaos. Oklahoma was first on the scene and its commanders were ready to battle the elements and the death and destruction left in Katrina's path and the worst flooding ever in a major city. What I learned in 2005 was that America has at its disposal the best weapon possible to throw at these adversaries—the National Guard.

COLONEL MIKE MCCORMICK
PIEDMONT

Oklahoma set a standard for joint operations between the Air and Army National Guard that was unparalleled in the history of civil relief operations. The logistical combat experience of an entire wing working hand in hand with talented and motivated Army National Guard soldiers provided a critical element of security and relief in a time of unprecedented natural disaster.

LIEUTENANT COLONEL MONTY BRODT
OKLAHOMA CITY

We provided stability to a devastated city without firing a single round at an individual or having a round fired against us. We rolled in and 99 percent of the people were absolutely ecstatic to see us there. They were glad to see someone try to stabilize the situation.

Almost every one of our soldiers had some type of skill that was needed for the unique domestic operation. That is why the National Guard is so much more valuable in such situations. On active duty, most troops are barely out of high school, or if they have been active for a decade, all they have done is their military job. On the other hand, a National Guard platoon sergeant may be a computer specialist, police officer, mechanic, electrician, plumber, or air conditioning expert. Most of the veteran Guardsmen bring a second, third, or fourth skill learned in the civilian world.

New Orleans was the craziest military operation I was ever part of. I saw things I have never seen anywhere else in the world. It was one of the most positive moments in the history of America's National Guard. If you take away the confusion of active duty forces that could not even carry loaded guns, it was the National Guard carrying the fight. It was General Wyatt and his troops providing law enforcement, search and rescue, and humanitarian relief while the 82nd Airborne was on television making the country feel better about itself. You can't blame them—that's where the media was. But it was our Oklahoma men and women who made the real difference in the wake of Hurricane Katrina.

CHAPLAIN (LIEUTENANT COLONEL) MICHAEL TAYLOR
BETHEL ACRES

We knew we were an important part of our nation's history. I had never seen a city with so many buildings setting in so much water in darkness. No light anywhere except what we could generate and from a full moon. And the city setting in water. It looked like tombstones. It looked like a graveyard. Like a city had died. That's what it looked like. It was a ghost town.

But through all that, our Oklahoma Guardsmen worked long and sweaty shifts in unimaginable conditions to perform their duties to fellow citizens. May their service never be forgotten.

COLONEL GREG FERGUSON
NORMAN

Katrina proved how effective communication between the Oklahoma Air Guard and Army Guard could result in such a seamless flow of troops, supplies, and equipment. The collaboration had to occur quickly because of the dire need. Air Guard operators sat at the same table with veteran Army Guardsmen and fit the pieces together. It is a testament to the kind of professionals we have in the Oklahoma National Guard, it is a testament to the high level of response possible even during a tumultuous time frame. We can do better next time, but I am eternally proud of the quality level at which we brought all our assets and expertise to bear.

CAPTAIN NATE MORGANS
TULSA

Our Guardsmen had a broad set of skills they could apply to a broad set of problems. Instead of just troops being ordered to "charge the hill," we literally took an infantry rifle company and asked them to set up an evacuation facility. They had all the civilian skills necessary to complete the mission. They had crazy guys like me who were firemen. My first sergeant worked at American Airlines. I had at least five officers and enlisted men who were police officers. There was nothing the group collectively could not do.

MAJOR LOUIS WILHAM
EDMOND

The National Guard has always been good about making stuff up as we go along. We can adapt, improvise, and change. Many of us took the horrible problems without an obvious solution as a challenge. Who would have envisioned a situation of where I'm trying to get ice or laundry contracts when there is no power for 20 miles in any direction? We overcame all obstacles by working together. We were flexible. We showed up on the ground and figured out how to do the best we could.

LIEUTENANT COLONEL MARK PILKINGTON
OKLAHOMA CITY

The legacy I took away from Katrina is that the National Guard always has to be flexible and we've got to be ready to go fast. I am so glad we never had to forcibly remove citizens from their homes even though the New Orleans mayor at one time ordered it. That would have perhaps crossed the line for the National Guard to take control over civil authorities. We must always respect that fine line between the military and civil government.

We learned a lot of lessons about building better communication structure, being able to talk to each other when all land lines and cell phone towers are inoperable. We also learned we weren't prepared with the right kind of maps to survey the problem and to keep up with what progress we were making.

Because we were helping fellow Americans, the feeling of reward was direct and more heartfelt. It's more authentic and easily understood by the troops under your command. You're helping out neighbors and that felt good.

STAFF SERGEANT ERIC WOLF
OWASSO

Oklahoma Guardsmen have served in two wars in the past two decades. But many guys talk about their mission in New Orleans more than missions to Afghanistan and Iraq. Katrina was the kind of mission you train for in the National Guard. Men and women don't join the Guard to go to a war in the desert, they join because they want to be involved in time of need for their fellow citizens. History will remember the professionalism and integrity of our Guardsmen who dealt with the most horrific disaster not even dreamed of by movie scriptwriters.

COMMAND SERGEANT MAJOR TONY RIGGS
NORMAN

There is no better reward than helping some elderly lady out of her house and into our truck, taking her to a location where she will be safe and fed. You can't replace that feeling. Oklahoma soldiers worked in three of the five parishes in New Orleans. It was a ghost town with stray animals running the streets. But through hard work and innovation, we gave peace to a city of chaos. Each day, we could tell the difference we were making. When we left the Big Easy, it was so much better than when we arrived.

CAPTAIN GERALD MASTIN
STILLWATER

Many of our young soldiers had to grow up quickly. Within a few days from leaving our civilian jobs we were carrying live ammunition and had the heavy responsibility of protecting life and property. Everyone pitched in. My first sergeant, Gary Davore, was a good motivator and handled any soldier that was homesick or traumatized by the human suffering we saw every day. Lieutenant Dan Lowery and Lieutenant Adam Courtright were my platoon leaders. They were young, but smart and quick learners. During those stressful times, the command structure of the National Guard was so meaningful. Veteran NCO's such as Sergeant First Class Darryl Kusher drew on their experience and helped the young guys in decisions that often had to be made in a matter of minutes.

FIRST LIEUTENANT CHRIS ISCH
EDMOND

You get a pretty good sense as a leader on a drill weekend of who are great and just good soldiers. But so much more can be gleaned in a long deployment. During Katrina, under Third-World country conditions, you see the soldier side of your men, the human side. For my troops, it gave me a better appreciation of them, to know that they would not complain because they gave such value to the job they were doing. It gave me a better appreciation for the role of the National Guard in the United States.

MASTER SERGEANT STEPHEN ROSEBROOK
MUSTANG

Did flying sorties around the clock make us better? Yes, it brought us back to our roots. We own the continental United States and everything within its border is ours to protect, provide, and support. That is what it brought back to me. The experience of Katrina made the National Guard as a whole better.

Our people were complexly sold on the humbling experience of being asked to save and rescue people who had no hope. We were thanked a million times—but we need to thank them. They brought our humanity back to us. Too often we get caught up in the mission mindset and forget the humanity side of our work. To bring these people back to life will always bring warmth to our hearts, no matter how long we serve in the Oklahoma National Guard.

FIRST LIEUTENANT FLOYD ROLAND
SHAWNEE

We went to New Orleans with a purpose that was three-fold. We tried to save and recover survivors. We tried to, in a very dignified manner, recover the remains of those killed. We tried to protect property. On a scale that no one had ever seen, we hit the ground to carry out our mission. I could see satisfaction on the faces of our troops when we left for home. They were tired and weary, but could hold their heads high with a sense of magnificent achievement.

SPECIALIST SCOOBY AXSON
OKLAHOMA CITY

While I was deployed with the Army National Guard in New Orleans, I gained a new respect for and a greater understanding of the value of the citizen soldier. Day after day, the unforgivable Louisiana heat beat down on thousands of soldiers. With no rain in the forecast and no sense of when they might go home, soldiers braved the humidity and sucked down gallons of water to try to stay hydrated.

The mission is simple for soldiers who serve our country and are called to duty. They do it, for whatever reason, so the average citizen does not have to. I will never forget a mother and father walk down the street with their two little kids in a shopping cart or water marks on houses for miles.

The price paid by citizen soldiers is a heavy one.

MAJOR JON GREENHAW
TULSA

All of us who helped in New Orleans and the Gulf Coast are proud that we went. It was a good and rewarding experience. In fact, it is perhaps the most rewarding experience of my life. Everyone stepped up in the whole process, but especially the crew chiefs. They worked the hardest watching out for us as we were landing and taking off. They took care of the passengers, sick people, and the never-ending job of loading aircraft after aircraft. They are the unsung heroes of our Katrina mission.

STAFF SERGEANT RICHARD DENNIS
TALALA

Often the little things still bring the most cherished memory of my service in the Katrina mission. When we refueled our Black Hawk, there were usually treats for the crew. We picked up extra boxes and gave them to evacuees as they were loaded on the helicopter for the trip out of New Orleans. It wasn't much, but a single piece of candy brought a smile to a face that had not seen joy for days. Some people thanked us left and right during the entire flight. But, it was our job. We felt more rewarded than they could ever imagine.

SERGEANT JENNIFER KORN
AGRA

My husband was crew chief on another aircraft so we were deployed at the same time. I left my mom at home with our five children. But that is a way of life in the National Guard. I am so proud we were able to go to help people in a neighboring state. It was hard to imagine water being over cars and halfway up bridges and overpasses. After a while, I was numb to seeing a refrigerator on top of someone's roof or a dead deer laying on the top of a submerged car.

I have thought many times of the danger we were in. Landing at the Superdome between light poles, trees, and power lines was crazy. Sometimes you would land and realize how dreadfully close you had gotten to something on the way down. But we had to do it—right then. Human lives depended on us doing the right thing quickly.

LIEUTENANT COLONEL CARLA WALKER
NORMAN

As a flight nurse, we lived at the New Orleans International Airport for several days. Army Guard helicopters brought us load after load of sick and injured people. One man died before we could get him on an airplane to safety. It was some of the hardest work any of us had ever done, both mentally and physically. It was so raw, but different than my civilian job as an emergency room nurse. A hospital ER is controlled. There was no control at the airport. You just saw raw human emotions and physical conditions that had been left to decay and deteriorate for days. All patients had an odor that permeated the air.

I am so glad I could help the people. I couldn't fix their lost homes, but I could at least fix what was there in front of me and take care of their immediate needs.

CHIEF WARRANT OFFICER 3
RICHIE SCHULER
MANNFORD

When I returned to the middle school classroom where I taught, I had to watch what I told inquiring students. I did not want to tell a seventh grader about caskets floating out of cemeteries. I did not want to tell them about the horrible shape people were in when we tried to fly them out of harm's way. Instead, I told them I had been gone for a month to help our neighbors in Louisiana and that I was proud to be in the National Guard. They understood my simple message and we moved on.

CORPORAL AMY LOHMANN
ALVA

No matter how difficult our task, it was all worth it for the people of the Gulf Coast. I was still in college when the deployment call came and I was a young mother. But I had an obligation to serve. When I arrived at the Superdome, people began begging me for water. I walked up on a young woman trying to clean her newborn baby. There were no diapers or any baby products. I just stopped in my tracks and was in shock. I won't ever forget that sight.

There was nowhere for people to go to the bathroom, so they found a corner in a huge crowd of people. No privacy whatsoever. Children with ripped clothing and babies in the sun for days wearing nothing but a diaper. I was devastated when a 12-year-old girl told me about gunshots, screams, and dead people she saw. I was honored to carry a ten-month-old baby to a waiting bus because his mother was too weak to carry him.

SPECIALIST TIMOTHY FARLOW
TULSA

I returned to New Orleans a decade after Katrina. I had a photograph taken of me under the same street sign in the French Quarter where I was photographed in 2005. It was surreal. It didn't look like the same place where we lived and served from a glass restaurant location. The trees had grown back. The big difference was the noise. During Katrina, it was eerily quiet. Now, there was lots of traffic and people walking everywhere. It was like I had never been there before.

CHIEF WARRANT OFFICER STONEY HOBBS
SAPULPA

The experience of Katrina gave me an appreciation for the simple things of life that we tend to lose sight of—food, clothing, and families. Every day we saw homes that were utterly destroyed, people waiting for food and water, and family members separated from each other.

I am so proud of the National Guard mission, to train a young man like me working at a grocery store to fly helicopters so that I could help people in need. I won't ever forget the unusual things about the mission. Frequently, alligators were in ditches along roads where we landed to pick up people. For an Oklahoma boy, it was something to fly almost anywhere in the area and see alligators.

SERGEANT MELANIE KERR
LUCIEN

Even if I had known what serving in New Orleans was going to be like, I would still say "yes" to the call to active duty. It was breathtaking when we first flew over the devastation. The flight crew lowered the back of the chopper so we could see better. Because of watching the news, we fully expected to land in the middle of a riot with blazing guns. Everyone was terrified. I prayed for my husband and children. I tried to mentally prepare myself for what could happen. We stepped off the chopper and I almost fell down with my 45 pounds of gear. It turned out to be horrific, but no shots were fired at us.

Another anxious time was when Hurricane Rita was passing. The tin roof on the building was lifting up. It made me miss home even more because in such weather I was used to snuggling with my husband or our babies to keep warm.

I would serve in the Katrina mission all over again. I don't take back any of it. I will always be ready to go and help people.

CAPTAIN CLIFTON BARGER
SHAWNEE

One of the scariest parts was the surge of aircraft two or three days into the mission. Control towers had been knocked out and there was no control procedure. We had to use our natural instincts as aviators to make corridors or highways in the sky. You had to be totally alert every moment. Aircraft were popping up between buildings and joining in the stream. They came from below and from the right and left. You would slow down so they could merge into this highway of helicopters in the sky.

CHIEF WARRANT OFFICER 3 CARLOS CASCANTE

We picked up water by the ton at makeshift airfields and dropped it in areas where it was needed. I didn't notice the long hours and awful conditions because I ran on adrenaline for the first three days. I felt good about what we were doing, but we talked and admitted we needed rest. There was little cell phone reception, but a short call home did wonders for morale.

In delivering Oklahoma soldiers to the Superdome after they heard reports of sniper fire and murders, I watched their eyes. They knew the seriousness of the situation. I told them, if you guys hear shots, please return fire, but please don't shoot up into the rotor system of the helicopter. Shoot down, not up. This was not the normal way of briefing troops, but we were doing it on the fly.

FIRST SERGEANT DANNY MATTHEWS
NORMAN

Getting rest during the first days of the mission was not a luxury, it was a necessity. It was so hot I was drained by the middle of the day. Once we landed that night, we had to preflight for the next day's mission. Once that was done and I sat down, I was gone. I was dead tired.

I felt a lot better flying troops to a mission that I could see was successful. Overseas, I might never know why we flew 600 troops to a certain place. But at home, as a National Guardsman on duty in a neighboring state, I could see the result of working so hard. It was immediate gratification.

SERGEANT SHAWN SMITH
TULSA

On a helicopter mission to a nursing home they made space for us to land in a tiny opening. Patients were lined up in order of how critical they were. There were no set rules, we had to operate by what seemed right at the moment. Patients were transported to the waiting chopper by grabbing blankets underneath them. When one blanket was about to get into the tail rotor, I pulled the blanket back and found a patient in terrible shape. We put five patients side-by-side on blankets in the back of the Black Hawk and flew them to the airport to get them out of New Orleans.

CHIEF WARRANT OFFICER 3
STEVE PHELPS
BROKEN ARROW

We finally got communications help to fly helicopters in the very busy airspace. An Air Force AWACS plane flew overhead and helped direct us and keep us out of other traffic patterns. As we got closer to downtown New Orleans, we were handed off to a ground unit that could send us to a particular nursing home or hospital or other rescue point. As a safety issue, especially because of the massive amount of air traffic, we ran daytime missions only. It was just a lot easier to see everything and operate in the daylight.

One of the most rewarding missions for me was to fly premature babies to safety from hospitals that had lost or were losing emergency power. The tiny victims had a fighting chance because of men and women of the Oklahoma National Guard.

SPECIALIST ANTHONY BALLONE
TULSA

Deployed at Hammond, Louisiana, was a blessing. Some people who owned a restaurant were so appreciative of what we were doing for Louisiana. They stayed open late for air crews and other personnel to come to a table full of jambalaya and red beans and rice. If the cooks left early, they gave me pots and pans of extra food for the late-arriving crews to have a hot meal. It was a nice gesture to go out and spend all day down there sweating to death in the mess and stench and to be able to have a nice meal and see someone smiling and saying, "Thank you."

FIRST LIEUTENANT MIKE KERR
CHANDLER

Each night's 8:00 p.m. briefing consisted of both good news and bad news. On one particular day, the forced-entry teams found nine corpses, 13 dogs, four cats, two birds, two rabbits, and two fish. The animals had all survived, making it a good day. The only shot heard that day was a Louisiana state trooper shooting the lock off a door.

The sights, sounds, and smell of the Hurricane Katrina response will never leave the memories of the Oklahoma National Guardsmen who answered the call to help their neighbors who could not help themselves.

SERGEANT ROCKY SEALS of Catoosa, one of the oldest soldiers in the Thunderbirds, took part in the fighting during the Tet offensive in the Vietnam War. He said:

I thought I had seen everything, but this was the worst. This was something that happened to part of our family. This is your own land, your own brothers and sisters.

As **MAJOR SCOTT HOUCK** of Norman reflected:

The real story of Katrina is the willingness of the citizen soldier to do extraordinary things under extraordinarily terrible conditions for American people. That is exactly what we are trained to do.

NATIONAL GUARD HEROES IN TASK FORCE OKLAHOMA

MEMBERS OF THE OKLAHOMA ARMY NATIONAL GUARD

ABERNATHY, TIMOTHY	ALLSEN, KENNETH L.	ARNEL, DARRYL R.	BAKER, GEORGE C.	BAROI, ROMEL S.
ABINAH, ANGELA S.	ALONZO, MICHAEL D.	ARNETT, JUSTIN M.	BAKER, JAMES P.	BARRETT, FRED L.
ACOSTA, ALEJANDRO L.	ANDERS, MARK I.	ARNOLD, JAMES B.	BAKER, JEREMIAH R.	BARRETT, RAY A.
ACOSTA, SILVESTRE R.	ANDERSON, ASHLEY L.	ARNOLD, LACYDE M.	BAKER, JEREMY S.	BARRETT, WESLEY W.
ADAMS, CHRISTOPHER J.	ANDERSON, DANIEL J.	ARVIZU, MARCELINO M.	BAKER, JOHN R.	BARRICK, BRADLEY J.
ADAMS, CLIFFORD T.	ANDERSON, DAVID M.	ASHCRAFT, KELLY D.	BAKER, JON P.	BARRICK, MATTHEW K.
ADAMS, ROBERT J.	ANDERSON, JASON M.	ASHLEY, FREDERICK B.	BAKER, EDWARD E.	BARROWMAN, STANLEY E.
ADAMSON, ERNEST L.	ANDERSON, JONATHAN S.	ASHMORE, JOHN T.	BAKER, JOSEPH A.	BARTEL, MARK E.
ADCOCK, SHELBY T.	ANDERSON, MICHAEL R.	ATKINSON, JAN M.	BALDWIN, JOSEPH A.	BARTELL, DANIEL R.
ADKINS, SAMANTHA A.	ANDERSON, MONTY L.	ATTAWAY, JACOB E.	BALFOUR, JARED A.	BARTON, RANDALL D.
AGUILAR, JEREMIAH D.	ANDERSON, NOAH H.	ATTEBERRY, CHRISTOPHER	BALL, WILLIAM A.	BASLER, BRETT D.
AGUILAR, JOE R.	ANDERSON, QUINCY E.	AUGUSTIN, CHRISTOPHER	BALLARD, LEMUEL R.	BASTEMEYER, MICHAEL E.
AIKEN, TILMON E.	ANDERSON, RICKEY L.	AULD, RENEE D.	BALLARD, RUSSELL L.	BATES, JASON S.
AIKIN, BOBBYE J.	ANDERSON, RYAN J.	AUSTIN, TOMMY D.	BALLARD, JOHN B.	BATSON, ROBERT T.
AKE, DUSTIN V.	ANDERSON, STEVEN R.	AUSTIN, WILLIAM J.	BALLENGER, ANDREW W.	BATTLES, SANDRA N.
ALARAFI, SAHAR S.	ANDERSON, LUCAS K.	AXSON, TERRY M.	BALLONE, ANTHONY S.	BAUSTERT, PAUL M.
ALBERS, ERIN M.	ANDERSON, PAUL M.	AXTON, JERRY E.	BANES, LEROY H.	BAWDEN, JOHN R.
ALBERT, JOSHUA B.	ANDERSONDARBY, GINA M.	AYERS, MATTHEW C.	BANNER, GROVER S.	BAXTER, MICHAEL D.
ALDERMAN, DAVID J.	ANDRES, JAMES W.	AYRES, RYAN B.	BARBEE, MANDEE L.	BAYHYLLE, BRIAN S.
ALEXANDER, FLOYD III	ANDREWS, JESSIE C.	AZBELL, LEWIS A.	BARGER, CLIFTON L.	BAYS, CHRISTOPHER E.
ALEXANDER, HUGH D.	ANTHONY, SLATON J.	BABCOCK, ROBERT W.	BARHAM, MICHAEL C.	BEACH, SEAN D.
ALEXANDER, JERRY D.	ANZALDUA, CHRISTOPHER	BACHER, DANNY W.	BARKER, DANIEL M.	BEAN, ANDREW T.
ALEXANDER, MICHAEL W.	APALA, ROBERT L.	BACON, JOSHUA W.	BARKER, DEWEY A.	BEASLEY, TIFFANY D.
ALLEN, BRIAN D.	ARCE, MARTIN R.	BAGGS, JASON L.	BARKER, KALVIN J.	BEAUCHAMP, BRIAN R.
ALLEN, DIRK J.	ARIAS, ALBERT P.	BAGWELL, BRIAN W.	BARNES, AL C.	BEAVERS, ROBERT W.
ALLEN, JOHN H.	ARIASFEO, JUAN I.	BAILEY, JOHN B.	BARNES, BENJAMIN G.	BECK, KEVIN O.
ALLEN, RANDY W.	ARIE, DEVIN W.	BAILEY, SCOTT A.	BARNES, JOHN E.	BECK, RONNIE A.
ALLEN, SAMMY D.	ARMSTRONG, MATTHEW W.	BAIR, RYAN T.	BARNES, MATTHEW W.	BEESLER, BOBBY E.
ALLEN, TIERRA T.	ARNDT, HEATHER A.	BAKER, CHRISTOPHER M.	BARNETT, JAMES T.	BEIER, RONALD E.
ALLMON, RYAN D.	ARNDT, JOHN W.	BAKER, GARY W.	BARNETT, KEELY N.	BELL, ANTHONY M.

BELL, DONAVAN T.
BELL, JASON L.
BELLVILLE, WILLIAM P.
BENEDICT, DANIEL R.
BENNETT, JAMES M.
BENNETT, KENNETH R.
BENNETT, LARRY P.
BENNETT, MELVIN C.
BENNETT, MICHAEL L.
BENNETT, STANLEY D.
BENNIGHT, JOSHUA A.
BENSON, JUSTIN D.
BENTLEY, ALLAN G.
BENTLEY, ALLEN J.
BENTLEY, DEREK A.
BENTLEY, TEDDY R.
BENTLEY, ROY L.
BENTON, TIMOTHY R.
BERG, MATTHEW J.
BERNSTEIN, BJ E.
BERRY, JOEL M.
BERRYHILL, TACIA L.
BERRYMAN, ANDREW S.
BERTOLAMI, DINA A.
BESHEARS, JASON D.
BETCHAN, MITCHELL L.
BETTINGER, DANIEL D.
BETTS, CHARLES R.
BEYE, DAVID J.
BIBLE, FRED L.
BICKERSTAFF, KRISTOPHER
BIER, BRANDON J.
BIGFEATHER, ROBERT B.
BIGGS, STEPHEN C.
BILLIE, DANNYE E.
BILLINGS, BROOKS A.
BILLUPS, JO A.
BILLUPS, THEODRE T.
BINGHAM, JOHNNY R.
BINKLEY, LYNUS L.
BISHOP, JASON W.
BISHOP, DAKOTA A.

BITTLE, JOSHUA J.
BLACK, DWIGHT E.
BLACK, JAMES C.
BLACK, KEVIN T.
BLACK, RONALD D.
BLACK, CRISTINA L.
BLACKBURN, SAMUEL C.
BLACKMAR, CHRISTOPHER
BLAIR, THOMAS J.
BLAKE, GARY J.
BLANCHARD, JEREMIAH G.
BLANK, WILLIAM L.
BLAYLOCK, MICHAEL D.
BLEVINS, SHANE C.
BLISS, MARDY R.
BLOSE, DONALD P.
BLOUNT, JARRED L.
BLOUNT, JASON E.
BLOUNT, JEFFERY D.
BLOUNT, JUSTIN L.
BLOXHAM, PHILLIP L.
BLUE, ERWIN K.
BLUEFRICK, WILLIAM A.
BOATENG, KWAHENA A.
BODDY, JOHN C.
BOHANNAN, LARRY E.
BOHLMAN, THERESE D.
BOLDING, DANIEL A.
BOLLES, CRYSTAL G.
BOLYARD, JEREMY D.
BOND, CHARLIE E.
BONDS, JAMES D.
BONE, MICHAEL D.
BONNER, DONALD H.
BONNETT, COURTNEY H.
BOOMER, BARRY C.
BOONE, TERRY A.
BOONE, KENNY J.
BOOTH, DAVID J.
BOOTH, JOSHUA C.
BOOTH, JOHN E.
BOOZE, CHARLES F.

BOOZE, JAMES W.
BOREN, JON P.
BORK, DOUGLAS G.
BORST, PHILIP A.
BOSTER, BOBBY W.
BOSTICK, KENNETH R.
BOSTWICK, MICHAEL D.
BOTTOMS, SCOTT L.
BOUCHARD, NICOLETTE C.
BOURLAND, THOMAS J.
BOURNE, BRANDON L.
BOWDEN, DARRELL L.
BOWEN, JANET L.
BOWEN, REX D.
BOWERMAN, JASON L.
BOWERS, KEVIN D.
BOWIE, JONATHON C.
BOWLES, ROKI A.
BOWLIN, RICHARD D.
BOWLING, CHRISTOPHER M.
BOX, JAY D.
BOYCE, SHAWN M.
BOYER, JOSHUSA B.
BOYKINS, ARCHIE L.
BOZARTH, JAMES E.
BRADFORD, RODNEY W.
BRADLEY, DEREK W.
BRADLEY, LANCE E.
BRADLEY, WILLIAM E.
BRADSHAW, BEAU D.
BRADSHAW, LYON E.
BRANDON, KEVIN M.
BRANHAM, DILLION J.
BRANNON, CODY T.
BRANSON, STANLEY J.
BRASEE, DONALD R.
BRAWLEY, RUBEN L.
BRAY, JASON M.
BRAY, JOHN M.
BRAY, GARY D.
BRECKENRIDGE, JAMIE L.
BREWER, CARL A.

BREWER, CHRISTOPHER J.
BREWER, NICHOLAS B.
BRIANT, JASON D.
BRICKER, MICHAEL T.
BRICKEY, MITCHELL L.
BRIGGEMAN, WILLIAM H.
BRIGGS, BYRON D.
BRIGGS, DALE R.
BRINKLEY, BRENT A.
BRINLEE, NORMAN J.
BRISCOE, JEREMY I.
BRISTOW, ROY W.
BRITE, ROBBY G.
BRITT, JAMES D.
BRITTENHAM, JOSHUA W.
BRITTON, JEFFREY D.
BROADHEAD, JUSTIN W.
BROCK, GENE F.
BROCKUP, DANIEL P.
BRODERICK, NATHAN J.
BRODT, MONTY L.
BROOKS, LINDSEY M.
BROOKS, MICHAEL D.
BROOMHALL, HOLLY M.
BROWN, DANIEL W.
BROWN, DAVID W.
BROWN, MATTHEW S.
BROWN, NILSON M.
BROWN, ROY E.
BROWN, ROYCE D.
BROWN, STEVEN C.
BROWN, JASON P.
BROWN, MARC A.
BROWNE, TERRY D.
BROWNING, MARRONE M.
BROYLES, ANTHONY H.
BRUECHER, MARSHALL B.
BRUMLEY, MARK N.
BRUNE, QUINTEN L.
BRUNER, DUSTINE S.
BRUNJES, JOHN D.
BRUNSON, JOHN M.

BRYAN, BILLY D.
BRYAN, MATTHEW S.
BRYANT, CARY T.
BRYANT, JEREMY W.
BRYANTJASON, K
BRYEN, JAMES L.
BRYIANT, ANDREW S.
BUCHANAN, DEXTER G.
BUCK, JAMES O.
BUCK, CHRISTOPHER L.
BUCKNERSTEPHEN, R
BULL, GARRY T.
BULLARD, CLAUDIA L.
BURDGE, JESSICA L.
BURGESS, MARK S.
BURGESS, SUMMER A.
BURK, PATRICK L.
BURKART, JOHN D.
BURKART, LUKE W.
BURKHART, WILLIAM R.
BURKS, JERRY R.
BURLEIGH, MATTHEW E.
BURLISON, AUTUMN N.
BURLISON, ERIC D.
BURNS, TY D.
BURRIS, HAROLD
BURRUS, STEPHEN K.
BURTCHER, JEFFERY D.
BUSH, JEFFREY S.
BUSSELL, JOSEPH P.
BUTLER, ALICE A.
BUTLER, KENNY F.
BUTLER, RICKY L.
BUTTS, CARNELL S.
BUTZ, PETER L.
BYAS, JACKIE L.
BYERS, JOSEPH E.
BYERS, MATTHEW R.
CABE, MICHAEL L.
CAFLIN, BRYAN P.
CAGLE, CHRISTOPHER M.
CAHILL, STEVEN B.

CAIN, CHARLES C.
CAIN, ODES III
CALDERWOOD, CHRISTOPHER
CALDWELL, STEPHEN D.
CALHOUN, MARQUISE E.
CALLENDER, RICKIE P.
CALVERT, ROSS P.
CALVEY, KEVIN J.
CAMERON, JOSEPH K.
CAMPBELL, FRANKIE A.
CAMPBELL, MARK A.
CAMPBELL, PAUL M.
CAMPOS, JARED A.
CANARD, DENNIS L.
CANTLEY, DONNA
CANTRELL, DAVID W.
CANTU, DANIEL
CANTWELL, KOREY L.
CAPSHEW, DUSTY D.
CARAWAY, CLINT C.
CAREL, DAVID P.
CARETTA, JOHN P.
CAREY, MICHAEL W.
CARGAL, DENNY R.
CARGILL, JOSHUA C.
CARLIN, GORDON E.
CARLSON, ANDREW J.
CARMAN, CHRISTOPHER D.
CARMAN, JAMES W.
CARMAN, CLINT E.
CARNES, RANDY K.
CARNEY, DUSTIN R.
CARNEY, LANCE R.
CARPENTER, JAMES E.
CARRELL, DOUGLAS K.
CARRISALEZ, ELLOID J.
CARROLL, JOHN H.
CARTER, BOBBY
CARTER, DAVID E.
CARTER, JEFFERY J.
CARTER, JONATHAN H.
CARTER, VERNON W.

CARTER, WOODROW W.
CARTER, FRANKLIN L.
CARTER, KENDALL L.
CARTER, STEPHEN R.
CARTY, JEFFREY W.
CARVER, DANNY D.
CASCANTE, CARLOS A.
CASH, ROCKY W.
CASKEY, SCOTT A.
CASSADY, ALEC S.
CASTILLO, MANUEL R.
CASTILLO, RUSSELL G.
CASTLEBERRY, THEIDIRE
CATES, JEREMY L.
CATO, VINCENT L.
CAULLEY, BRANT E.
CAVIN, JAMES F.
CAVIN, WILLIAM J.
CHAFFIN, DEREK T.
CHANEY, BENNY R.
CHANEY, MONICA L.
CHAPMAN, JAMES H.
CHAPPELL, TONY M.
CHARLES, BUFORD F.
CHAROONSAK, ERIC J.
CHASE, AMOS M.
CHASE, COLLIER S.
CHASE, TONYA D.
CHASTAIN, BARRETT A.
CHASTAIN, LARRY M.
CHASTAIN, JAMES P.
CHASTEEN, DAVID K.
CHEATWOOD, RUSSEL C.
CHEEK, JAY B.
CHERRY, WILLIAM T.
CHESBROUGH, KENNETH A.
CHESSER, KENDON J.
CHESTNUT, SHANE A.
CHILDERS, BRIAN K.
CHILDRESS, WILLIAM G.
CHIN, RODERICK G.
CHISHOLM, FRANK E.

CHISUM, TODD E.
CHITWOOD, JAMES E.
CHOMOSH, CHRISTOPHER
CHRISMAN, JOHNATHAN W.
CHRISTENSEN, WALTER A.
CHRISTIAN, GARRETT T.
CHRISTINE, ALEXANDER J.
CHRISTY, ANDREW R.
CHRISTY, MICHAEL D.
CHUDOBA, CHADWICK M.
CHUTE, ALLEN R.
CIRGENSKI, JOSEPH S.
CLARK, ANTHONY K.
CLARK, GERALD W.
CLARK, JOSHUA R.
CLARK, WILLIE L.
CLARY, BRUCE R.
CLAYTON, KENNETH M.
CLEPPER, AMANDA D.
CLEWIEN, EDWARD M.
CLIMER, LONNIE D.
CLOUTIER, KIMBERLY K.
COBB, CALEN J.
COBERLY, DALON L.
COBLE, ROBERT K.
COCHRANE, GABRIEL A.
CODY, JAMES C.
COE, ADAM B.
COFFMAN, CHARLES M.
COLE, ADAM G.
COLE, JOSEPH A.
COLE, AARON J.
COLE, JOSHUA L.
COLEMAN, KENNETH M.
COLLETT, BLAKE A.
COLLETT, JOSEPH C.
COLLIER, TERRY S.
COLLINS, ANTHONY H.
COLLINS, CHAD E.
COLLINS, DANNY L.
COLLINS, DEMPSEY M.
COLLINS, DOUGLAS W.

COLLINS, HAROLD W.
COLLINS, JAMES C.
COLLINS, MERLE D.
COLLINS, WILLE L.
COLON, ANTHONY
COLONEY, ANDREW S.
COLSON, JARED C.
COLWILL, BENJAMIN L.
COMBS, CHRISTOPHER D.
COMSTOCK, LEVI G.
CONANT, JOSHUA E.
CONDE, CORK W.
CONDIT, JACK W.
CONDIT, RYAN M.
CONDREY, CURTIS W.
CONFORTI, KEVIN P.
CONLEY, CARL W.
CONLEY, JAMES A.
CONNELLY, DAVID R.
CONNER, MICHAEL E.
COOK, CHRISTOPHER J.
COOK, DUSTIN J.
COOK, KEITH P.
COOK, ROBERT L.
COOK, SEAN L.
COOPER, DANNY K.
COOPER, DENNIS R.
COOPER, RUSSELL A.
COOR, HOUSTON L.
COPELAND, HOWARD D.
COPLEY, DAVID B.
CORBIN, WILLARD H.
CORTEZ, PEDRO JR.
CORTRIGHT, ADAM C.
COSTILOW, PAUL D.
COTTON, LARRY G.
COUNCILL, REBEKAH S.
COURANGE, JEREMY P.
COWAN, DAVID S.
COX, CLAY C.
COX, JAMES M.
COX, MICHAEL L.

COX, TYREL A.
CRABTREE, ROGER J.
CRAFT, MCKINLEY D.
CRAIG, DIANA D.
CRAIG, MARVIN M.
CRAIG, TY S.
CRAIN, JORDAN E.
CRAM, DAVID A.
CRAMER, JONATHAN D.
CRANE, CHARLES R.
CRAPO, STANLEY M.
CRASE, MICHAEL E.
CRAWFORD, HOWARD E.
CRAWFORD, ZACHARY G.
CRAWFORD, BARRY T.
CRAWFORD, JOEL D.
CREAGER, GORDON A.
CREASON, KENNETH B.
CREEKMORE, CHRISTOPHER
CRENSHAW, JACKIE D.
CRENSHAW, LARRY J.
CRENSHAW, JASON C.
CREUTZ, PATRICK C.
CRIDER, KENNETH R.
CRILE, BART A.
CRITES, ERICK W.
CRITES, JACOB L.
CRITES, PRESTON D.
CROFT, ROBERT D.
CROSBY, GARY L.
CROSBY, LARRY G.
CROSBY, ROBERT D.
CROSS, DOUGLAS R.
CROSS, HAROLD R.
CROSS, PHILLIP D.
CROSS, WILLIAM D.
CROSS, ROBERT W.
CROSSLAND, RICKY W.
CROTTY, THOMAS L.
CROUCH, WILLIAM J.
CROUCH, KEVIN L.
CROW, MICHAEL L.

CROWDER, PATRICK W.
CUADERES, CHARLES C.
CUDD, KENTON R.
CULLISON, CHRISTOPHER
CULVER, CHRISTY L.
CUMMINS, CHRIS L.
CUNNINGHAM, JERRY W.
CUNNINGHAM, ROBERT J.
CURRIER, KELBY D.
CURTIS, ALVIN R.
CURTIS, BARRY W.
CURTIS, DAVID B.
CURTIS, DENNIS A.
CURTIS, KENNETH C.
CURTIS, CHARLOTTE G.
CURTIS, JANE L.
CUSHER, DARRELL L.
CUSHMAN, ROGER L.
DAGE, DONALD D.
DAHLKE, WILLIAM S.
DALE, MICHAEL W.
DALLAS, CLINTON A.
DANIELS, KENNITH R.
DANNELS, GREGORY J.
DANNER, MERRILL K.
DANSBY, RYAN K.
DARTER, LARRY D.
DAVENPORT, JAMES T.
DAVIDSON, TIMOTHY R.
DAVIS, ANTHONY D.
DAVIS, CLINTON L.
DAVIS, CRYSTAL B.
DAVIS, DAVID H.
DAVIS, DAVID L.
DAVIS, DAVID N.
DAVIS, GERALD W.
DAVIS, GREGORY D.
DAVIS, KENNETH L.
DAVIS, LARRY L.
DAVIS, MAJOR D.
DAVIS, MICHAEL K.
DAVIS, NICHOLAS T.

DAVIS, RANDY L.
DAVIS, RUSSELL E.
DAVIS, SHANTEL R.
DAVIS, TIMOTHY JR.
DAVIS, DENNY E.
DAVIS, ELI G.
DAVIS, JASON T.
DAVIS, LARRY K.
DAVIS, PAUL E.
DAVISON, RODNEY F.
DAY, JOE H.
DEATON, JEFFREY D.
DEBOUGH, LEE P.
DEBROECK, DANIEL J.
DECKER, TERRY A.
DEERING, MYLES L.
DEHART, BOBBY J.
DEJESUS, VALENTIN
DEKLE, LESLEY L.
DELANEY, JEFFERY M.
DELANGEL, VICTOR H.
DELCOUR, RAYMOND E.
DELEON, JULIO A.
DELEON, MANUEL III
DELINE, LINDSAY B.
DELOZIER, MATTHEW D.
DELSO, JOHN P.
DELUA, CARLOS P.
DEMERY, BRYANT A.
DENAEYER, DANIEL G.
DENEEN, MICHAEL J.
DENNIS, OREN J.
DENNIS, RICHARD E.
DENNIS, SHANNON B.
DENTON, DUSTIN R.
DENTON, BENJAMIN D.
DENTON, DAVID L.
DERROW, MARK D.
DERRYBERRY, RODNEY D.
DERYCKERE, DOUGLAS E.
DESEYN, CHARLES J.
DESHAZO, BRIAN S.

DESOTEL, JOSHUA L.
DEVORE, GARY L.
DEWEESE, TREVOR A.
DIACON, JOHN D.
DICKENSON, LINDA S.
DIEL, CURTIS D. JR.
DIETRICH, PAUL A.
DIETZEL, NATHAN S.
DILLARD, DARNELL E.
DILLON, CHRISTOPHER C.
DILLS, LONNIE S.
DINWIDDIE, BRENT H.
DISMORE, LARRY R.
DIXON, RICHARD K.
DIXON, RONALD D.
DIXON, EDDIE L.
DOBBS, AIRON R.
DOBBS, CARROLL E.
DOBRY, BRENT L.
DOBSON, DOUGLAS B.
DOBSON, KYLE P.
DOBSON, SEAN M.
DODD, GARY W.
DODSON, JAMES C.
DODSON, WILLIAM T.
DOGGETT, JOHN W.
DONAGHUE, ROBIN K.
DONALDSON, VINCENT E.
DONATHAN, JERRY L.
DONES, ANGEL M.
DONOVAN, DAVID L.
DOOLEY, CLINTON W.
DOREY, RICKEY A.
DORRIS, BRANDYN L.
DORSEY, GARRY L.
DORSEY, VANNA M.
DOUGHERTY, AARON T.
DOUGHTY, JAMES A.
DOUGLAS, JAMES H.
DOUGLAS, KELVIN A.
DOUGLAS, SAMANTHA R.
DOURS, AMANDA K.

DOUTHITT, CALEB C.
DOUVILLIER, RALPH A.
DOW, DANIEL R.
DOW, JOSHUA N.
DOWDLE, TERRY L.
DOWELL, KIRT S.
DOWNARD, KIMBERLY D.
DOWNING, ADAM D.
DOYLE, RICKY C.
DOZAL, JOSE L.
DREILING, CLIFTON W.
DRURY, KENNETH M.
DUCHARME, MELISSA D.
DUDLEY, DALE M.
DUFF, MICHAEL C.
DUJARDIN, RICHARD G.
DUKE, BRANDON E.
DUNAGAN, CHRISTOPHER L.
DUNAWAY, AARON B.
DUNBAR, DUSTIN W.
DUNCAN, BRIAN L.
DUNCAN, CISSY L.
DUNCAN, LANCE A.
DUNCAN, LONNIE K.
DUNCAN, REX E.
DUNCAN, SHANE B.
DUNCAN, JUSTIN S.
DUNGAN, CHRISTOPHER J.
DUNHAM, GORDON T.
DUNLAP, RUSSELL W.
DUNN, BENJAMIN A.
DUNN, ERIC W.
DUNN, JOHN R.
DUNSON, MICHAEL L.
DUPREE, CLINTON E.
DUPREE, TANNER L.
DURBIN, JOSEPH K.
DURBIN, KELLIE J.
DURHAM, STACIE K.
DUROY, MICHAEL C.
DUSTIN, JOSEPH L.
DUTTON, CHARLES T.

DUTY, RONALD G.
DUVALL, MARC A.
DUVALL, DANNY A.
DYER, BRANDON L.
EADES, LEWIS C.
EAKINS, RICHARD H.
EARHART, DAVID P.
EARLS, JASON W.
EASLEY, HEATHER L.
EASLEY, JOSEPH F.
EASLEY, DARRYL R.
EASTIN, CHAD A.
EAVES, CARL D.
ECCLES, HOHN R.
ECK, JUSTIN L.
EDDY, TLISA L.
EDGAR, WILLIAM T.
EDGETT, JANESSA J.
EDWARDS, BRADLEY A.
EDWARDS, REBECCA N.
EDWARDS, TERRANCE R.
EDWARDS, WILLIAM A.
EDWARDS, FRANK W.
EDWARDS, MATTHEW L.
EEDS, STEVEN D.
EFIRD, JOSEPH R.
EIKLOR, MARY A.
EISENBERGER, BILL J.
EISENHAUER, DAVID E.
ELDER, ALLEN H.
ELDER, JOSHUA L.
ELDRIDGE, KEVIN R.
ELIX, LIONAL C.
ELKINS, JERRY W.
ELLIOTT, ERICK S.
ELLIOTT, GARY L.
ELLIOTT, NATHAN P.
ELLIS, GARY E.
ELLIS, JASON S.
ELLIS, RYAN D.
ELLIS, WILLIAM L.
ELLIS, STEVEN R.

ELLISON, ADAM W.
ELLISON, CHAD A.
ELLISON, FLETCHER G.
ELLISON, JAMES F.
ELLISON, MATTHEW J.
ELLISON, WILLIAM C.
ELLISON, THOMAS L.
ELLYSON, WILLIAM W.
ELMORE, CHRISTOPHER W.
ELMORE, JONATHAN D.
ELMORE, LESTER W.
ELVIK, TERRY J.
EMERSON, ERIC M.
EMMERT, BRIAN D.
ENBLOM, ERIC P.
ENGEL, BRIAN C.
ENGLAND, BILLIE E.
ENGLISH, DAVID G.
ENGLISH, KEVIN L.
ERICKSON, CORINNA Y.
ESCOE, RICHARD L.
ESPINOZA, GERMAN JR.
ESPINOZA, OSBALDO
EUBANKS, BOBBY J.
EVANS, BOBBY J.
EVANS, JOANNE K.
EVANS, KRIS L.
EVANS, ROBERT D.
EVANS, TAYLOR S.
EVANS, ALEXANDER C.
EVANS, DALE V.
EVERETT, JEDIDIAH A.
EWING, BRADLY E.
FAIRCHILDS, KENNETH J.
FARBER, JASON A.
FARBES, JOSHUA M.
FARISS, CHRISTOPHER S.
FARLEY, ROGER P.
FARLOW, TIMOTHY J.
FARMER, JASON M.
FARMER, LEVI G.
FARNEY, TIMOTHY M.

FARRAR, RODNEY T.
FARRIS, JARED R.
FARRIS, JEFFERSON R.
FAULKNER, WILLIAM B.
FAZEKAS, BURT L.
FEES, KODY D.
FEICHO, ANDREW G.
FENN, GEORGE D.
FENTON, LARRY J.
FERGUSON, THOMAS E.
FERRELL, STANTON T.
FEUERBORN, GREGORY C.
FIELDER, ANDREW W.
FIELDS, LATOYA R.
FIELDS, TONY L.
FIELDS, WILLIAM L.
FIRESTONE, AMY L.
FITZGERALD, JEREMY D.
FITZGERALD, PATRICK T.
FITZSIMMONS, JOHN W.
FLAHERTY, TYLER D.
FLANAGAN, EARL W.
FLEER, BRANDI J.
FLEER, ROBERT D.
FLEISHMAN, LAWRENCE I.
FLETCHER, JOSHUA R.
FLETCHER, MANDY L.
FLORES, JUAN C.
FLOWER, JEDD M.
FLOWERS, DONNA L.
FLOWERS, JEREMY S.
FLOYD, RODNEY G.
FOGLE, TYLER D.
FONVILLE, KEVIN C.
FOOR, PATRICK M.
FORD, CHRISTOPHER R.
FORD, JEFFERY W.
FORD, SHAWN W.
FOREMAN, RHONDA K.
FORSTER, PETER R.
FORTNER, TROY J.
FOSS, JARED R.

FOSTER, CODY F.
FOSTER, DENVER W.
FOSTER, DONALD R.
FOSTER, STEPHANIE L.
FOSTER, TRAVIS E.
FOSTER, TREVOR J.
FOUNTAIN, WALTER E.
FOUST, ROY G.
FOUTCH, LARRY E.
FOWLER, CHRISTOPHER E.
FOWLER, DEREK W.
FOX, FORREST D.
FOX, KAREY L.
FRAIRE, THOMAS
FRANCIES, FREDERICK G.
FRANCIS, JEFFERY S.
FRANCIS, CELIA C.
FRANDSEN, DONALD I.
FRANKLIN, JONATHAN R.
FRANKS, BILLY J.
FRASURE, DONOVAN J.
FRAZIER, ERIC W.
FRAZIER, WILLIAM A.
FREEMAN, CLARENCE M.
FREEMAN, KENNETH J.
FREI, ROBERT H.
FRENCH, CHRISTOPHER J.
FRENCH, MARK A.
FRIDAY, FRED W.
FRIESE, ERIC J.
FRITCHIE, CALVIN D.
FRIZZELL, MATTHEW G.
FROMM, KEVIN P.
FROST, DUSTIN L.
FRY, BRANDEN D.
FRY, BRYON D.
FRY, JARRED N.
FRYE, TRACY E.
FULGHUM, MARSHALL V.
FULK, JAMES E.
FULLER, SHEPPARD P.
FULLER, DANIEL M.

FULTON, TREA B.
FUNCK, JOSEPH W.
FUNK, JUSTIN L.
FUNK, BRANDON S.
FURMAN, DARRYL A.
GABBERT, DUSTIN W.
GAGE, BRIAN K.
GAINES, TARESSA R.
GAINES, STEVEN R.
GALAN, PHILLIP
GALLAGHER, JOHN D.
GALLOWAY, SHERRI L.
GAMBILL, ERIC L.
GAMMON, GREGORY T.
GARDNER, FLOYD E.
GARDNER, STEPHEN D.
GARNER, TODD L.
GARRETT, KEVIN D.
GARRETT, NICOLE S.
GARRISON, BENJAMIN P.
GARRISON, LUKE T.
GASTON, BRYON R.
GASTON, HUGH L.
GATLIN, DAVID S.
GATZ, CHAD A.
GATZKE, ROBERT W.
GATZKE, RUSSELL W.
GAUTHIER, TRAVIS J.
GAYLER, DONALD D.
GAZA, ROBERT I.
GEE, STACEY D.
GEISINGER, PAUL A.
GENTRY, MICHAEL S.
GEORGE, BRADLEY S.
GEURIN, TERI K.
GIBSON, LOUIS G.
GIBSON, STEPHEN B.
GIBSON, TIMOTHY W.
GIFFORD, BENNY J.
GIFFORD, MILES B.
GILBERT, THOMAS S.
GILBERT, TIMOTHY F.

GILCREST, KELLY A.
GILL, JAMES P.
GILLIAM, DANNY M.
GILLILAN, WELDON A.
GILLILAND, MATTHEW P.
GILLUM, JOSHUA W.
GILMORE, JOSEPH F.
GILMORE, TAWNY M.
GILPIN, SEAN A.
GILREATH, JARED D.
GLASGOW, KYLE N.
GLASS, ROBERT T.
GLIMP, RUSSELL A.
GLISSON, KYLE R.
GOAD, TOMMIE L.
GODINEZ, SARAH J.
GODWIN, EDWARD A.
GODWIN, REGINA F.
GOEBEL, GARY L.
GOKEY, MARTIN E.
GOLDEN, DANNY E.
GOLDEN, KENNETH R.
GOLDESBERRY, JOSHUA P.
GOLDSBERRY, JOHN S.
GONZALES, ANNA M.
GONZALEZ, DANIEL J.
GONZALEZ, GUSTAVO A.
GONZALEZ, JESSE J.
GOODBALLET, JOSEPH E.
GOODCHILD, STEVEN J.
GOODMAN, WENDY A.
GOODNIGHT, KEVIN S.
GOODWIN, JAY R.
GOODWIN, WESLEY R.
GOODWIN, BILL J.
GORACKE, MICHAEL S.
GORDON, AMY K.
GORDON, CHRISTOPHER A.
GORDON, FERRELL W.
GORDON, MICHAEL W.
GORDON, RAY D.
GORDON, WILLIAM J.

GORDON, JAMES L.
GORE, JIMMY L.
GORRIN, GREGORY W.
GORTON, JASON T.
GOSNEY, BRIAN M.
GOSNEY, LANCE G.
GOSS, JASON D.
GOTT, RONALD L.
GOURD, JOHNSON C.
GOWDY, RANDALL L.
GOZA, WILLIAM C.
GRAGERT, DOUGLAS T.
GRAHAM, DOUGLAS W.
GRANGE, SHAUN R.
GRAVES, JONATHAN P.
GRAVES, MATTHEW D.
GRAVES, ROBERT D.
GRAVES, SAMUEL P.
GRAY, CHARLES D.
GRAY, WILLIAM R.
GRAY, JAMES H.
GRAYSON, KENNETH L.
GRAYSON, SHIRLEY M.
GREEN, DANIEL H.
GREEN, ISRAEL
GREEN, JORDAN M.
GREEN, JUSTIN V.
GREEN, KEITH W.
GREEN, LARRY G.
GREEN, MICHELLE R.
GREEN, RODNEY K.
GREEN, ROBERT C.
GREENFIELD, BRANDON J.
GREENFIELD, JAMES L.
GREENHAW, JON R.
GREER, MICHAEL T.
GREGORY, JONATHAN S.
GREGORY, PHILLIP D.
GRENN, STEVIE L.
GRIFFIN, CLAYTON W.
GRIFFIN, DONALD E.
GRIFFIN, JEREMY D.

GRIFFIN, VANICE M.
GRIFFIS, JOHN M.
GRIFFIS, WARREN R.
GRIFFITH, GARY L.
GRIFFITH, RAYMOND S.
GRIFFITH, KYLE R.
GRIMES, CORBIE N.
GRIZZLE, CHRISTOPHER W.
GROTTS, JUSTIN B.
GUERRERO, DAVID
GUERRERO, DICK G.
GUEVARA, JUAN A.
GUINN, MITCHELL E.
GUINN, CHAD D.
GUINN, WILLIAM D.
GURLEY, WESLEY A.
GUTTERY, RICK M.
GUYTON, JERRELLE D.
GWIN, JESSICA R.
HACKER, RICKIE A.
HACKETT, STANLEY R.
HACKNEY, CHRISTOPHER L.
HACKWORTH, JASON L.
HADDOCK, JENNIFER L.
HADDOX, JOE B.
HADRAVA, BRADY J.
HAGELBERG, LARRY W.
HAGEMEIER, JEREMIAH J.
HAGER, JOHN J.
HAGER, RYAN M.
HAHN, BELVA J.
HAHN, VINSON L.
HAINES, TERRY R.
HAINES, JOE A.
HAINES, JOSEPH C.
HAIRELL, DAVID L.
HALE, JEFFERY P.
HALE, MICHAEL J.
HALE, RUSSELL A.
HALE, TERRY C.
HALES, CHRISTOPHER R.
HALES, PHILLIP C.

HALL, ANTHONY P.
HALL, JEREMY M.
HALL, TIMOTHY D.
HALL, TREVOR E.
HALL, WARREN K.
HALL, ZACHARIE W.
HALLEY, DAN R.
HALLMARK, TERAH S.
HAMBLIN, JONATHAN D.
HAMILTON, CHRISTOPHER
HAMILTON, DANIELLE L.
HAMILTON, JOSHUA L.
HAMILTON, MICHAEL S.
HAMMER, TIMOTHY D.
HAMPTON, ROBERT R.
HAMPTON, SHANE R.
HANCOCK, JAMES E.
HANCOCK, JONATHAN R.
HANNA, WILLIAM B.
HANNAH, TRACI L.
HANNAN, JONATHAN A.
HANSEL, DWIGHT E.
HANSEN, CHARLES J.
HANSON, MELVIN Y.
HARDEN, CLIFFTON R.
HARDIN, ANDREW N.
HARDIN, LANDON K.
HARDIN, WILLIAM D.
HARDIN, WILLIAM D.
HARDING, BRIAN A.
HARDMAN, CARLTON B.
HARKEMA, FRANCIS W.
HARLAN, ERIC W.
HARMAN, JASON W.
HARP, RICHARD A.
HARPER, ANTHONY T.
HARRELL, EDDIE W.
HARRELL, ROBBY T.
HARRELL, TIMOTHY C.
HARRIS, AARON J.
HARRIS, CAREY E.
HARRIS, CHRISTOPHER J.

HARRIS, MATTHEW D.
HARRIS, MONICA L.
HARRIS, MORIAH D.
HARRIS, NICK A.
HARRIS, PAUL J.
HARRISON, ERNEST T.
HARRISON, SHAD C.
HARSHA, MATTHEW J.
HART, JASON E.
HART, JOHN M.
HART, STEVEN A.
HARTER, BRYAN M.
HARTIN, JASON F.
HARTLINE, JAMES G.
HARVEY, TRAVIS G.
HASTEY, REX L.
HASTINGS, QUENTIN D.
HASTINGS, JAMES S.
HATFIELD, PATRICK B.
HATTER, TIMOTHY M.
HAUBERT, JAMES M.
HAUENSTEIN, DANIEL R.
HAUGHT, FLOYD D.
HAUGHT, TYRIE D.
HAVENS, CHRIS L.
HAWK, JOHN W.
HAWKINS, COREY D.
HAWKINS, ROBBY L.
HAWKINS, WILLIAM R.
HAWS, MICHAEL L.
HAXTON, ROBERT L.
HAYES, DONNELL JR.
HAYES, RONNIE A.
HAZEN, AARON M.
HEALEY, SHERMAN R.
HEARN, DAVID R.
HEFLIN, DUSTON M.
HEIDERSTADT, NICHOLAS
HEILAMAN, AARON S.
HEINE, NICHOLAS X.
HEITMAN, WALTER L.
HELMER, JEREMY S.

HELMS, JOE A.
HENDERSON, BRYAN D.
HENDERSON, DEANDRE L.
HENDERSON, GARY R.
HENDERSON, SAMUEL A.
HENDRICKS, JOHN H.
HENDRICKS, MARTY L.
HENNINGER, JEFFREY A.
HENRY, JASON A.
HENRY, JOSEPH A.
HENRY, SEAN M.
HENSLEY, STEPHEN W.
HEREDIA, LUIS D.
HERMAN, PHILLIP K.
HERNANDEZ, JOHN K.
HERNANDEZ, KATHRIN E.
HERNDON, MATHEW C.
HERRERA, FRANCISCO
HERRMANN, CALVIN D.
HERZER, TIMOTHY J.
HESSON, DANIEL R.
HESTON, JAMES N.
HEWETT, JUSTIN L.
HEWETT, KYLE B.
HEYNE, KENNETH E.
HICKERSON, JOHN M.
HICKS, CHARLES W.
HIGDON, RYAN L.
HIGGINBOTHAM, ERIKA R.
HIGHT, JAMES E.
HIGHTOWER, HUGH E.
HILL, BRENT P.
HILL, BROCK
HILL, RICHARD A.
HILL, TAKORYA T.
HILL, THOMAS C.
HILL, KYLE B.
HILL, ROBERT B.
HILL, WILLIAM E.
HILLIAN, PAUL D.
HILLIARY, JACKIE E.
HIMES, CHRISTOPHER R.

HINCH, BRADLEY C.	HORNER, VANESSA K.	ILIFF, JARRETT C.	JOHNSON, ALVIN E.	JONES, WESLEY A.
HINES, MICHAEL S.	HORTON, FRANK M.	IMPSON, ANDREW S.	JOHNSON, CHRISTOPHER W.	JONES, WILLIAM W.
HINES, RICHARD A.	HOSKINS, JOSEPH D.	INCIARTE, RAMIREZ R.	JOHNSON, DUSTIN G.	JONES, SCOTT A.
HINSHAW, LUCAS D.	HOUCK, BRANDON W.	INGRAM, CORY D.	JOHNSON, ESTER P.	JONES, STEWART M.
HINTON, JASON R.	HOUCK, SCOTT M.	INGRAM, SEAN W.	JOHNSON, JAMES E.	JORDAN, DAVID L.
HISE, TONY G.	HOUK, CHRISTINA M.	ISBILL, ROWDY B.	JOHNSON, JAMIE A.	JORDAN, JACOB W.
HOBBS, STONEY W.	HOWARD, NICHOLAS J.	ISCH, CHRISTOPHER K.	JOHNSON, JIMMY G.	JORDAN, JOHN D.
HOBBY, DELBERT R.	HOWARD, BOBBY G.	ISHAM, TRACY A.	JOHNSON, JIMMY V.	JORDAN, JOHNNY R.
HOBSON, JOHN W.	HOWE, DAVID G.	IVERSON, JASON R.	JOHNSON, JOHN C.	JORDAN, SIDNEY L.
HOCKENSMITH, DAVID W.	HOWELL, DERWIN R.	IVERSON, KENNETH S.	JOHNSON, KEITH E.	JUMP, PAUL W.
HOCKER, DEE P.	HOWELL, TIMOTHY S.	IVES, ROBERT W.	JOHNSON, RICHARD L.	JUSTUS, JEFFREY W.
HODGES, CHARLES M.	HOWENSTINE, SEAN E.	IVES, ROBERT W.	JOHNSON, RICKY L.	KANADA, AARON M.
HOGAN, DANNY W.	HOWHARD, GALE C.	IVIE, RICKY L.	JOHNSON, ROBERT C.	KANE, CLAYTON S.
HOHRMAN, TIMOTHY W.	HUBBARD, RYAN C.	IVY, JAMES J.	JOHNSON, RONALD W.	KANNARD, MICHAEL S.
HOLDER, NANCY A.	HUCKABAY, AARON S.	IZER, DOUGLAS T.	JOHNSON, RYAN D.	KANNEMAN, NICHOLAS A.
HOLDGE, ODIS D.	HUCKABEE, DAVID C.	JACK, KENNETH E.	JOHNSON, RYAN T.	KAPPLE, DAVID K.
HOLLAND, ERIC D.	HUDDLESTON, CARLOS A.	JACKSON, BENNETT R.	JOHNSON, SHAWN E.	KAY, ROBERT M.
HOLLAND, JIM D.	HUDGINS, AARON W.	JACKSON, BERNARD W.	JOHNSON, TODD M.	KEATING, DAVID L.
HOLLE, WILLIAM M.	HUDSON, MARTY D.	JACKSON, CLIFFORD D.	JOHNSON, ANDREW H.	KECK, COLBY L.
HOLLON, LISA M.	HUDSON, STEVEN A.	JACKSON, DALE W.	JOHNSON, MICHAEL E.	KEENAN, RAYMOND N.
HOLMAN, CURTIS JR.	HUFFMAN, JESSE M.	JACKSON, DAVID R.	JOHNSON, MICHAEL P.	KEENER, CHADD W.
HOLMAN, GERALD D.	HUGHART, MATTHEW W.	JACKSON, HUGH D.	JOHNSTON, JARROD D.	KEENER, STEPHANIE D.
HOLMAN, JACKIE D.	HUGHES, KEVIN D.	JACKSON, SHAWN E.	JOLLEY, RANDALL S.	KEHN, BRANDI N.
HOLMES, JACOB L.	HUGHIE, BUDDY J.	JACKSON, JASON R.	JOLLY, KERRY L.	KEITH, BRYAN J.
HOLSTEN, TODD K.	HULSEY, JESSE W.	JACOX, JOSHUA A.	JOLLY, WALTER S.	KELLEY, STEVEN L.
HOLT, ALBERT C.	HUMPHREY, JONATHAN C.	JACQUET, JOHN M.	JONES, ANDREW P.	KELLOGG, DAVID D.
HOLT, EDDIE W.	HUNT, RUSSELL L.	JAGGERS, MARSHALL W.	JONES, BILLY S.	KEMNITZ, RICKIE D.
HONEYCUTT, NATHAN C.	HUNT, NATHAN W.	JAIME, ELISA C.	JONES, BRADLEY D.	KEMP, FINLEY B.
HOOD, JOSHUA E.	HUNTLEY, ROBERT A.	JAMISON, ANDREW W.	JONES, CHAD R.	KEMPER, JUDITH A.
HOOK, GARY D.	HUPP, ROY S.	JANSEN, RICHARD K.	JONES, CHRISTOPHER H.	KENDALL, DONNA K.
HOOPER, CASEY L.	HURLEY, SCOTT C.	JANUARY, MICHAEL P.	JONES, DARRELL W.	KENDRICK, STEPHEN K.
HOOPER, MONTGOMERY P.	HURST, KURT A.	JARNAGIN, KYLE P.	JONES, DAVID M.	KENDZIERSKI, LAMONTE M.
HOOTEN, CODY K.	HUSSENIN, KHALID K.	JARVIS, JOSEPH B.	JONES, DILLON E.	KENNEDY, ERIC C.
HOOVER, DANNY J.	HUTCHINS, ERIC J.	JASPER, BRIAN D.	JONES, EDDIE G.	KENNEDY, RICHARD L.
HOPKINS, CHRISTOPHER J.	HUTCHINS, JOHN A.	JEFFERSON, ROBERT W.	JONES, JAY L.	KENT, NATHAN A.
HORN, DAKOTA J.	HUTCHINSON, EMMANUEL M.	JENKINS, LAWRENCE P.	JONES, JUSTIN S.	KENYON, ELIZABETH A.
HORN, MICHAEL A.	HUTTON, BRIAN T.	JENKINS, SARA S.	JONES, MAHALIE J.	KEOUGH, KARL W.
HORN, TERRY L.	HYDEN, JERRY D.	JENNINGS, GEORGE R.	JONES, MARION K.	KERCHEE, JEFFREY R.
HORNBACK, DAVID S.	HYMEL, JOSHUA D.	JENSEN, STEVEN L.	JONES, MARK D.	KERR, CASEY M.
HORNBERGER, RICHARD T.	HYSLOP, JAMIE R.	JIMENEZ, HILARIO	JONES, NICHOLAS K.	KERR, DANIEL P.
HORNE, JAMES E.	HYSLOP, JOHNNY D.	JOERN, JERRY E.	JONES, RICHARD A.	KERR, MELANIE F.
HORNER, JOHNNY A.	IGLESIAS, JEREMY L.	JOHNS, JEREMY A.	JONES, RICKEY L.	KERR, MICHAEL R.

KERR, RICHARD E.	KORN, BRUCE N.	LAWSON, RICHARD D.	LOGAN, JON M.	MALDONADO, JOSELYN
KERR, ROCHELLE F.	KORN, JENNIFER E.	LAY, MATTHEW C.	LOGAN, MARION E.	MALLORY, JONAS R.
KESTER, JIMMIE E.	KRAPCHA, EDWARD L.	LAZEAR, DANIEL L.	LOHMANN, AMY D.	MALLORY, TAMELA J.
KETCHER, JON W.	KRAUTLARGER, BRANDON L.	LEA, JERRY D.	LOMBARD, KELLEY L.	MALONE, ANGEL L.
KETCHER, JOSEPH D.	KRIEGH, MICHAEL A.	LEAL, DONNIE R.	LONDON, JEFFREY H.	MAMMEDATY, MONTE R.
KETCHUM, CASEY J.	KRISE, STEPHEN J.	LEATHERS, RANDY S.	LONEY, CHRISTOPHER N.	MANCINO, NICHOLAS C.
KETCHUM, RUSSELL S.	KRITTENBRINK, JOSEPH A.	LEATHERWOOD, CHRISTOPHE	LONEY, ANTHONY D.	MANCINO, THOMAS H.
KEYES, JOSEPH F.	KRIWANEK, JAMES B.	LEDBETTER, BRIAN K.	LONG, ERIC R.	MANGHAM, AMBER R.
KIELTY, YEVONNE M.	KRUSE, RICHARD L.	LEDFORD, MICHAEL D.	LONG, CHARLES W.	MANIER, SPENCER L.
KILE, ANTHONY M.	KUEHNY, JOHN H.	LEDFORD, JIM M.	LONGFOUCHER, MATTEA R.	MAPES, JEFFREY L.
KILGORE, DARA L.	KUHLMAN, ADAM S.	LEE, CURTIS R.	LONGORIA, LARRY L.	MAPLES, RICHARD E.
KILLINGSWORTH, BRANDEN	KUKUK, CHRIS M.	LEE, KEVIN R.	LOONEY, MATTHEW H.	MARACARA, JORDAN M.
KILLMAN, CHARLES J.	KUNKEL, BRUCE E.	LEE, WILLIAM F.	LOOSE, JOHN C. JR.	MARCHANT, KENNETH R.
KIMBERLIN, DOUGLAS M.	KURTZ, CHRIS E.	LEE, ANTHONY S.	LOSSON, WILLIAM K.	MARCY, JOHN H.
KIMBLE, KORY D.	KUTZ, JON M.	LEFORCE, DANIEL C.	LOUIS, ROCHELL D.	MARINARI, JUSTIN M.
KIMBREL, BRANDON L.	KVARME, ROLAND K.	LEFTWICH, WILLIAM E.	LOVEDAY, TRAVIS L.	MARK, KURTTIS A.
KIMBRELL, JERRY D.	KYLE, MICHAEL W.	LEGGETT, JEFFERY J.	LOWE, MICHAEL A.	MARKS, LISA E.
KIME, ROGER A.	LACOUR, CARLOS E.	LEGLER, GEOFFREY J.	LOWRY, JAMES D.	MARLER, TONY L.
KINCHEN, VAN L.	LACY, CHRISTOPHER L.	LEHRMAN, BRANDON L.	LUBBERS, LYLE G.	MARLER, WILLIAM J.
KING, CHAD A.	LAFRANCE, TERRY M.	LEIRD, DUSTIN L.	LUCAS, BENJAMIN L.	MARQUIESS, DUSTIN A.
KING, DUSTYN L.	LAMPSHIRE, MARION S.	LENARD, MICHAEL L.	LUGO, JESUS JR.	MARRINER, BRUCE W.
KING, RICHARD B.	LANCE, JOHN D.	LENERTZ, ADAM R.	LUIS, CASEY J.	MARSH, JARED W.
KING, SHAMEKA L.	LAND, JEREMIAH A.	LESLIE, COURTNEY B.	LUNA, DENNY K.	MARSH, ROBERT F.
KING, SHANE J.	LANE, GEORGE L.	LEVOIT, JONATHAN K.	LUNA, TIMOTEO R.	MARSHALL, LLOYD W.
KING, TERRY L.	LANE, SAMUEL E.	LEWIS, JACOB D.	LUSTY, ROBERT B.	MARSHALL, TUI T.
KING, TIMOTHY L.	LANE, STEVEN D.	LEWIS, BOBBY R.	LUTTRELL, RALPH T.	MARSHALL, RANDALL E.
KING, AARON R.	LANE, ROBERT C.	LEWIS, ZACHARY P.	LYLES, AARON J.	MARSTON, LUTHER R.
KING, SAMMY J.	LANEY, BRIAN S.	LIGHTFOOT, JEFFREY A.	LYNCH, TERESA A.	MARTIN, DAVID S.
KINSEY, ANTHONY R.	LANHAM, NUBBIN L.	LIGHTFOOT, NATHAN S.	LYON, DERRICK E.	MARTIN, ERIC A.
KINSEY, RANDY W.	LANKFORD, DEREK R.	LINDAMOOD, COLBY C.	MACENTIRE, BRADLEY D.	MARTIN, JASON S.
KINSLER, CLIFFORD A.	LANKFORD, DUSTY D.	LINDEMANN, BRAD A.	MACKEY, DAVID W.	MARTIN, MATTHEW P.
KINTSEL, JOEL G.	LANKFORD, GEORGE W.	LINDGREN, ANDREW B.	MADDUX, JIMMY C.	MARTIN, REX A.
KIRKPATRICK, THMOTHY D.	LANKFORD, MATTHEW D.	LINDSAY, GARY R.	MADEWELL, WILLIAM J.	MARTIN, RICK L.
KIRKPATRICK, WILLIAM J.	LAQUA, FRANK M.	LINDSEY, STANLEY L.	MAEZ, JASON L.	MARTIN, TIMOTHY L.
KITCHELL, DEBBIE S.	LARIGEY, KENNETH R.	LINN, JEFFREY B.	MAGGARD, JOHN R.	MARTIN, JAMES T.
KITCHENS, CHAD A.	LARRICK, BRADLEY A.	LINSE, MICHAEL K.	MAHAN, JAMEE A.	MARTINEZ, ANGELO T.
KLINGAMAN, SCOTT D.	LASHLEY, KARL B.	LITTLE, JOSEPH S.	MAHAN, JAMES A.	MARTINEZ, SALVADOR E.
KNIGHT, DAVID E.	LAWHON, MATTHEW A.	LIVELY, ROGER E.	MAHONEY, KEVIN M.	MASON, ADAM L.
KNIGHT, JACOB R.	LAWRENCE, GEORGE W.	LIVESAY, DAVID F.	MAI, BRIAN J.	MASON, CLAY D.
KNOLES, GAREY D.	LAWSON, SEAN B.	LLOYD, CHRISTOPHER J.	MAIB, KENNETH L.	MASON, JAMES C.
KOCH, BROOK S.	LAWSON, JEFFREY M.	LLOYD, ROBERT W.	MAJORS, BRANDON R.	MASON, MARION N.
KOEHLER, CHRISTOPHER R.	LAWSON, JOSHUA D.	LOCHMANN, SAMUEL J.	MAKINS, DALE A.	MASON, SANDRA D.

MASTERS, MICHAEL A.
MASTIN, GERALD E.
MATHENY, AARON M.
MATHENY, SHANNON T.
MATHERLY, DAVID D.
MATHEWS, ROBERT W.
MATHISON, DAVID R.
MATKIN, AARON L.
MATLOCK, CHRISTINA N.
MATLOCK, JEFFREY T.
MATTE, LUCIEN J.
MATTHEWS, DANNY R.
MATTHEWS, MICHAEL T.
MATTHEWS, CHRISTOPHER
MAUCH, ANGELA D.
MAVIS, DANIEL J.
MAXWELL, BENJAMIN M.
MAY, DOUGLAS W.
MAY, ELMO D.
MAYS, MICKEY R.
MAYS, RALPH D.
MAZUR, ROBERT A.
MBELU, STEPHANIE N.
MCANALLY, KEVIN R.
MCANELLY, JESSE L.
MCBRIDE, JASON L.
MCCAIN, EDDY H.
MCCALL, JARED W.
MCCALLISTER, TYRELL L.
MCCART, RUSTY D.
MCCARY, MALACHI S.
MCCLAIN, DENNIS T.
MCCLAIN, ROGERETTA T.
MCCLINTICK, SUSAN A.
MCCLUNG, DUSTIN E.
MCCONKAY, CULLEN E.
MCCONNELL, CLIFFORD R.
MCCONNELL, DAVID D.
MCCOY, MATTHEW D.
MCCRIGHT, PATRICK D.
MCCUBBIN, STEPHEN N.
MCCUISTION, JUSTIN K.

MCCURLEY, MICHAEL L.
MCDANIEL, JUSTIN J.
MCDANIELS, RODNEY D.
MCDONALD, MATTHEW S.
MCDONNAL, JAMES C.
MCDUFFIE, BRIAN R.
MCELHANEY, JOSEPH D.
MCELLIGOTT, MAXWELL N.
MCFADDEN, JOHN H.
MCFARLAND, MARK E.
MCFARLIN, BEAU J.
MCFARLIN, CHRISTOPHER
MCGARY, REBECCA G.
MCGEE, JASON T.
MCGEE, NICHOLAS J.
MCGEHEE, SHAWN R.
MCGLOCKIN, ARBELO J.
MCGOLDEN, BRIAN K.
MCGOWAN, GREGORY K.
MCGUFFEE, JEFFREY L.
MCGUIRE, BRANDON S.
MCHENRY, KELVIN L.
MCINTIRE, JAMES S.
MCINTIRE, DANIEL C.
MCKAMIE, MICAH W.
MCKEE, JOSHUA L.
MCKEE, JOSHUA E.
MCKEE, NICKOLAS A.
MCKEEVER, SHERRIE L.
MCKENNA, SEAN P.
MCKENZIE, CHRISTOPHER
MCKEOWN, MATTHEW P.
MCKEOWN, PHYLLIS L.
MCKIDDY, MICHAEL D.
MCKINLEY, WILLIAM A.
MCKINZIE, LORN C.
MCKINZIE, MARK A.
MCLAUGHLIN, SCOTT D.
MCMAHAN, CLINTON R.
MCMILLIN, CHANSEY L.
MCNAC, STEVEN K.
MCNAIR, DAVID R.

MCNAMAR, BRANDON B.
MCNEELY, WILLIAM C.
MCNEELY, KEVIN L.
MCPHERSON, ERICH C.
MCVICKER, CHRISTOPHER
MCWETHY, CHRISTOPHER P.
MEADOWS, JONATHON C.
MEANS, WILLARD E.
MEARES, JEREMY R.
MEARS, JOHN C.
MEDINA, GUSTAVO
MEEK, PATRICK F.
MEEK, STEVEN D.
MEEK, JOHN W.
MEEKS, JACKIE L.
MEEKS, PHILLIP N.
MEGET, JARED G.
MEGLI, RODNEY V.
MELOY, CURTIS J.
MERKLE, JOSEPH A.
MERLEY, MELVIN C.
MERRIFIELD, CHRISTIAN
MERRIOTT, ROBERT W.
MERRITT, DOUGLAS W.
METCALFE, PAUL A.
METTE, CABRINA L.
METZ, DEREK L.
METZGER, DANIEL A.
MEYERS, JEREMY G.
MICHAELIS, ADAM J.
MILAM, BENNY D.
MILAM, CHRISTOPHER T.
MILAM, DONAVAN T.
MILLEDGE, JOSHUA M.
MILLER, BRIAN L.
MILLER, BRUCE J.
MILLER, CAMERON E.
MILLER, CHARLES L.
MILLER, CHRISTOPHER L.
MILLER, CHRISTOPHER S.
MILLER, CLIFFORD J.
MILLER, GLENN E.

MILLER, JAMES E.
MILLER, JOHN B.
MILLER, KENNETH R.
MILLER, MATTHEW C.
MILLER, PHILIP R.
MILLER, RICHARD G.
MILLER, SCOTT A.
MILLER, THERIN Q.
MILLER, TRAVISE L.
MILLER, TROY S.
MILLER, VINCENT E.
MILLER, DERICK M.
MILLER, WILLIAM R.
MILLS, BENJAMIN C.
MILLS, JARED T.
MILSTEAD, PHILIP N.
MIMS, WILLIAM N.
MITCHELL, BRIAN D.
MITCHELL, DENNIS R.
MITCHELL, JASON A.
MITCHELL, JUSTIN T.
MITCHELL, MICHAEL E.
MITCHELL, SAMUEL K.
MITCHELL, THOMAS C.
MITCHELL, DAVID W.
MITCHUSSON, SCOTT L.
MIZE, BOBBY W.
MIZE, DAMON A.
MOEN, BRADLEY G.
MONTE, GERALD P.
MONTGOMERY, CHRISTOPHER
MONTGOMERY, TRAVIS J.
MOODY, DENNIS D.
MOONEY, DEBRA K.
MOORE, ALEXANDER C.
MOORE, CORY R.
MOORE, DANIEL W.
MOORE, JAMES P.
MOORE, KENNETH M.
MOORE, LOYD E.
MOORE, MICHAEL C.
MOORE, MICHAEL D.

MOORE, NICHOLAS D.
MOORE, ROHDNEY W.
MOORE, SHAUN A.
MOORE, TRISHELL M.
MORALES, HECTOR H.
MORDECAI, EDWARD T.
MORDECAI, RONNIE G.
MORGAN, VANCE L.
MORGAN, JACOB E.
MORGAN, MICHAEL S.
MORGANS, NATHAN A.
MORREAU, DAVID R.
MORRIS, CHANTRY S.
MORRIS, JAMES R.
MORRIS, JESSE R.
MORRIS, LUSHENA S.
MORRIS, CHRISTOPHER L.
MORRISON, CHRISTOPHER
MORRISON, JERRY W.
MORRISS, MICHAEL A.
MORRISSEY, BRANDON M.
MORROW, MICHAEL C.
MORSE, BRANT L.
MOSCATELLO, VINCENT L.
MOSELEY, JIMMIE L.
MOSHER, ALLEN B.
MOSHER, ROBERT R.
MOSLEY, PAUL W.
MOSS, MAX E.
MOTLEY, LAURA L.
MOYER, AARON R.
MUGELE, BRADLEY M.
MULLIN, HAROLD D.
MULLINS, MARTY
MUNDY, STEVEN M.
MUNHOLLAND, GREGORY D.
MUNSEY, SHANE D.
MURDOCK, NATHAN R.
MURPHY, WILLIAM F.
MURPHY, GREGORY B.
MURRAY, DANIEL
MURRAY, DERRICK J.

MURRAY, DAVID F.
MURRY, WADE I.
MUSGROVE, JACK D.
MUSTIN, LARRY R.
MYERS, GERALD JR.
MYERS, JOHN T.
MYRDA, JOSEPH A.
NADER, CHRISTOPHER M.
NAGEL, KENNETH E.
NAIL, DONALD J.
NAILS, CHRISTOPHER C.
NALIN, JAMES M.
NANTZ, ROBERT J.
NAPIER, JOSHUA C.
NEAL, BROOKE L.
NEASE, TRAVIS W.
NEE, RHONDA L.
NEECE, AUBREY D.
NEESE, ASHLEY F.
NELMS, DONALD L.
NELSON, BRIAN S.
NELSON, DANIEL J.
NELSON, DAVID L.
NELSON, DESIREE N.
NELSON, RONNIE A.
NELSON, TIMOTHY D.
NEUMANN, JASON W.
NEWBERRY, JENNA M.
NEWCOMB, CORY M.
NEWMAN, FRANK M.
NEWMAN, JESSE I.
NEWMAN, KEITH W.
NEWMAN, TIMOTHY J.
NGOTNGAMWONG, ADAM C.
NIBBS, DELENA M.
NICHOLLS, BRUCE A.
NICHOLS, ADAM R.
NICHOLS, JERRY D.
NICHOLS, KEVIN J.
NICKEL, BRIAN D.
NICKELL, BRADLEY S.
NICKLES, JAMES M.

NIEHOFF, KEVIN D.
NIELSEN, EDWARD K.
NIPPER, DANIEL K.
NISSEN, NATALIE S.
NIX, GARY D.
NIX, JEREMY J.
NIX, LEE F.
NIXON, STEVEN P.
NOBLE, ROBERT C.
NODINE, MARK A.
NOLAN, LAVERA V.
NORMAN, CHAZ B.
NORMAN, JESSE K.
NORRIS, JOSEPH S.
NORRIS, WILLIAM E.
NOTTINGHAM, BILLY R.
NUNEMAKER, KENNETH R.
NUTTY, BRADLEY N.
OAKES, MICHAEL D.
OAKS, DWIGHT, C.
OBANION, SHANNON D.
OBRIEN, JUSTIN R.
OCONNELL, THOMAS J.
ODOM, GEORGE R.
OGLESBEE, JOHN A.
OGWIN, CHRISTOPHER W.
OKEY, MICHAEL R.
OKU, OGBO E.
OLDHAM, JUSTIN M.
OLEARY, CHARLES S.
OLINGER, JOSHUA M.
OLIVER, CLAUDE C.
OLIVER, DANIEL G.
OLIVER, JENNIFER D.
OLIVER, KATHLEEN N.
OLIVER, MARILYN M.
OLIVER, VICTOR A.
OLSEN, ERIC W.
OLSON, JON H.
OLVERA, ANTONIO G.
ONEAL, CHAD A.
ONEAL, EDMUND G.

ONEAL, ERNEST W.
ONEILL, PHILIP J.
ONEILL, TODD M.
ONEY, JUSTIN W.
ONTIVEROS, PATRICK E.
ORTIZ, RICHARD T.
ORTIZQUINTANA, SIGFRID
OSBORN, DUSTIN D.
OSBORNE, MICHAEL E.
OSTERHOUT, STEVEN L.
OTEY, CHRISTOPHER M.
OTTEN, JAMES L.
OVERBY, SHANE J.
OWEN, KIRK A.
OWEN, DALE L.
OWENS, KIM E.
OWENS, LARON H.
OWENS, MARCUS K.
OWENS, MARTY A.
OWENS, RICHARD B.
OWENS, SCOTT B.
OWENS, JAMES J.
OXENFORD, JEREMY T.
OXFORD, JUSTIN D.
PACE, TIMOTHY G.
PAGE, JOHN R.
PAGE, JOSHUA G.
PAINTER, KEVIN A.
PALMER, AARON M.
PALMER, TIMOTHY C.
PANDO, OCHOA A.
PANGLE, DUSTY A.
PANTOJA, JUAN J.
PARHAM, RODNEY
PARISOTTO, EDWARD M.
PARK, GREGORY L.
PARKER, BRADLEY J.
PARKER, DANIEL A.
PARKER, DAVID A.
PARKER, JUSTIN L.
PARKER, TIMOTHY A.
PARKINSON, FRANK A.

PARKS, BRANDON K.
PARKS, DEREK B.
PARKS, CHARLES A.
PARMELEE, JOHN K.
PARMELEE, PATRICIA K.
PARO, TIMOTHY W.
PARRISH, CHAZ R.
PARSONS, WILLIAM K.
PASON, MATTHEW P.
PATKOWSKI, MAX D.
PATTERSON, ACE D.
PATTERSON, JASON W.
PATTERSON, JEFFERY E.
PATTERSON, MICHAEL S.
PATTERSON, RUBY E.
PATTERSON, REBECCA M.
PATTON, SAMUEL S.
PAULK, JASON C.
PAWLOWSKI, DOMINIC L.
PAWNEE, AARON J.
PAXSON, JOHNNY L.
PAYNE, BILLY J.
PAYNE, JASON G.
PAYNE, JIMMIE W.
PAYNE, PAUL L.
PAYNE, BILLY R.
PAYNE, JUSTIN T.
PEACOCK, KEIRON B.
PEACOCK, STEVEN W.
PEAK, STEVEN D.
PEARCE, BRENT E.
PEARSON, PATRICK D.
PECK, BRYAN E.
PECK, TODD W.
PEDERSEN, RODNEY A.
PEELER, NATHAN B.
PEERY, DAVID M.
PENA, JESSE J.
PENDLETON, JAMES P.
PEOPLES, BUTURM T.
PEREZ, CHRISTOPHER F.
PERKINS, JIMMY W.

PERKINS, JUSTIN E.
PERSHICA, JERRY L.
PETERS, RICHARD W.
PETERS, TIMOTHY L.
PETRY, STEVEN D.
PETTIT, CHRISTOPHER A.
PHELPS, STEVEN J.
PHILLIPS, ADAM C.
PHILLIPS, CORY G.
PHILLIPS, DANNY R.
PHILLIPS, HOMER F.
PHILLIPS, PATRICK W.
PHILLIPS, QUINTON J.
PHILLIPS, ROBERT D.
PHILLIPS, STEVEN T.
PHILPOT, BRIAN L.
PHILPOT, MARCUS H.
PHILPOT, STEVEN E.
PHIPPS, JAMES D.
PICKERING, AMANDA M.
PICKETT, DANIEL H.
PIERCE, NICHALOS B.
PIERCE, SHAWN A.
PILKINGTON, MARK A.
PINCKNEY, MELISSA D.
PINDEL, RICHARD E.
PINEDA, RICARDO A.
PINEIRO, ROBERT A.
PINGLETON, BRIAN D.
PINGREY, JEFFREY F.
PIPHER, TYLER J.
PIRTLE, JAMES C.
PITTMAN, E H.
PITTS, CAMERON W.
PLATT, ROBERT W.
PLATTE, KARL W.
PLEAS, AARON
PLUMLEE, ERIK D.
PLUNKETT, SHERLESE A.
POE, MARK A.
POGUE, BRYAN T.
POLK, WILLIAM H.

POLLOCK, HERSHELL F.
PONDER, MICHAEL D.
PONTIER, NATHAN P.
POOL, GARY L.
POOLAW, MICHAEL D.
POOLAW, RODERICK L.
POOLER, JASON M.
POPE, ERICA D.
PORTER, JAMES M.
PORTER, SAMMY L.
PORTERFIELD, JUSTIN R.
POTTER, DAVID A.
POTTER, GRANT L.
POTTER, MEGAN K.
POTTS, BOBBY R.
POTTS, JUSTIN W.
POTTS, JOEL M.
POWELL, JOSHUA M.
POWELL, WILLIAM E.
POWELL, WAYNE L.
POWERS, SHAWN F.
PRATER, BARRY G.
PRESCOTT, CARL E.
PRESTON, VERNON D.
PRINCE, JAMES C.
PRINCE, MYCAL L.
PRITCHETT, TIMOTHY A.
PRIVITT, RICHARD L.
PROCK, MICHELLE L.
PROCTOR, JEREMY D.
PROCTOR, ROBERT J.
PRUITT, JOSEPH E.
PRYOR, MATTHEW C.
PUCLIK, TIMOTHY J.
PULIS, MATTHEW A.
PULLINS, BRANDON D.
PUNDSACK, ANTHONY C.
PURCELL, ROBBY L.
PURDUE, NATHAN L.
PURSIVILLE, FRANKLIN D.
PURZER, CHRISTOPHER A.
PUTNAM, JOSHUA V.

PYLE, CARL H.
QUAID, JESSE V.
QUALLS, KEVIN A.
QUINN, DAVID L.
QUINN, JEREMY A.
QUINTANILLA, VICTOR W.
RAASCH, DANIEL W.
RABY, RICHARD D.
RACKLIFF, DENA M.
RADEMACHER, WILLIAM G.
RAGAN, JOHNNY N.
RAGLAND, RONALD B.
RAHLF, JUSTIN M.
RAMBO, MARCUS E.
RAMIREZ, CHARLES J.
RAMIREZ, CHRISTOPHER L.
RAMIREZ, SEAN M.
RAMIREZ, TONY A.
RAMIREZ, GEORGE C.
RAMOS, ERIK A.
RAMOSNIEVES, MIGUEL A.
RAMSEY, JAMES R.
RAMSEY, MATTHEW E.
RANDALL, JON C.
RANDALL, MATTHEW J.
RANDALL, AARON G.
RANDOLPH, DAVID M.
RANDOLPH, GREGORY T.
RANKIN, NICKOLAS J.
RANNEY, ERIC D.
RAPER, AMANDA A.
RAWLS, CHARLES E.
RAY, ERIC S.
RAYL, SCOTT A.
READ, NICHOLAS B.
REDEAGLE, COURTNEY D.
REDINGER, CORY L.
REED, BILLY R.
REED, CASEY D.
REED, CHRISTOPHER T.
REED, LEONARD L.
REED, MICAH B.

REED, STEVEN D.
REEL, MARK S.
REES, NATHANIEL M.
REEVES, JACOB R.
REID, WILLIAM P.
REID, WARREN F.
REIKOWSKY, MATTHEW B.
REMPE, CHRISTOPHER C.
RENAUD, LONNIE D.
RENFRO, LARRY D.
RENFROW, JEREMY D.
RENTIE, JOSEPH M.
REQUA, STEPHANIE J.
REYES, DEE W.
REYES, RALPH D.
REYNOLDS, AMANDA R.
REYNOLDS, GEORGE L.
REYNOLDS, JACKIE G.
REYNOLDS, JASON W.
REYNOLDS, MARK S.
REYNOLDS, MATTHEW E.
REYNOLDS, TOMMY L.
REYNOLDS, WESLEY J.
RHINE, TINA A.
RHOADS, JORDAN R.
RHODES, SCOTTY S.
RHODES, STEPHEN E.
RICE, SHARON K.
RICHARD, JAYON J.
RICHARDS, CHESTER R.
RICHARDS, JIMMY H.
RICHARDS, JULIE D.
RICHARDS, NATHAN D.
RICHARDSON, BRANDON L.
RICHARDSON, JAMES L.
RICHARDSON, JONATHAN E.
RICHMOND, BUELL D.
RICHTER, NATHAN D.
RICKETTS, THOMAS A.
RIDLEY, KENNETH M.
RIGGINS, RICHARD A.
RIGGS, DELL E.

RIGGS, KEVIN J.
RIGGS, LEON W.
RIGGS, RAYMOND B.
RIGGS, ROBERT E.
RIGGS, TONY F.
RILEY, ADAM E.
RILEY, DARRELL E.
RILEY, GEOFFREY N.
RILEY, MICHAEL S.
RINEHART, JEFFREY L.
RING, LEO F.
RIOS, NANCY
RITTENHOUSE, BRADLEY D.
RITZMAN, GREGORY L.
RIVAS, CHARLES E.
RIVAS, MANUEL I.
RIVERA, JOE JR.
RIVERA, MICHEAL A.
RIVERA, JOSHUA
RIVERS, BRIAN A.
ROBBINS, CHRISTOPHER N.
ROBBINS, NOEL D.
ROBERSON, BRETT W.
ROBERSON, CHRISTOPHER
ROBERSON, CHRISTOPHER
ROBERSON, BRYAN T.
ROBERTS, IAN S.
ROBERTS, LLOYD W.
ROBERTS, STEVEN M.
ROBERTS, TROY A.
ROBERTS, WADE A.
ROBERTS, JOSHUA T.
ROBERTSON, BARRY L.
ROBERTSON, MATTHEW B.
ROBINSON, CRAIG M.
ROBINSON, DANIEL W.
ROBINSON, DARRELL T.
ROBINSON, GABE L.
ROBINSON, GARY T.
ROBINSON, JOHN W.
ROBINSON, KENNETH D.
ROBINSON, SHAAN P.

ROBISON, BILLY R.
RODGERS, GORDON S.
RODRIQUEZ, GUADALUPE F.
ROE, CHARLES E.
ROE, ROBERT C.
ROED, KEVIN D.
ROGERS, ADAM J.
ROGERS, ALLEN R.
ROGERS, DAVID A.
ROGERS, JOE D.
ROGERS, KENNETH G.
ROGERS, STEPHEN D.
ROGERS, WILLIAM K.
ROLAND, FLOYD K.
ROLAND, RANDY L.
ROLLOW, DAVID A.
ROMAN, VICTOR C.
ROMERO, JOY L.
ROMESBURG, SHAWN E.
ROOT, CHRISTOPHER L.
ROSE, JAMES R.
ROSE, MICHAEL D.
ROSE, MICHEAL S.
ROSHELL, ROBERT W.
ROSS, HOWARD E.
ROSS, JONATHAN E.
ROSS, TODD A.
ROSSI, JAVIER M.
ROTH, MICHAEL J.
RUCK, JAMES J.
RUCKEL, ROBERT M.
RUCKER, TRAVIS L.
RUDD, BRIAN A.
RUDY, ELIZABETH R.
RUEB, DANIEL S.
RUFFIN, MARK A.
RUIZ, ALBERT III
RUMPLE, WALTER J.
RUSSELL, JEREMY D.
RUSSELL, LOGAN M.
RUSSELL, MICHAEL G.
RUSSELL, GORDON P.

RUTZ, PHILLIPS J.
RYERSON, LANCE A.
SABRSULA, LEE R.
SADBERRY, EDDIE L.
SALAS, TONY
SALAZAR, MATTHEW A.
SALAZAR, MATTHEW J.
SALDANA, JOSE E.
SAMPLE, TERRI L.
SAMSEL, LAUREN M.
SAMUELS, KYLE A.
SANCHEZ, ADAM L.
SANCHEZ, ROBERT L.
SANCHEZ, RUBEN S.
SANDERS, CHANCE E.
SANDERS, JOHN W.
SANDERS, LARRY A.
SANDERS, RICHARD K.
SANDERS, ROLLAND W.
SANDERS, SCOTT D.
SANDERS, VERNON R.
SANDERS, WILLIAM M.
SANDERS, CHARLES E.
SANDERS, JACKIE D.
SANDERSFIELD, JAMES E.
SANDERSFIELD, JOHN E.
SANDERSON, JEFFERY T.
SANDFUR, BENNY E.
SANDOVAL, MICHAEL D.
SANMILLAN, WILLIAM J.
SANTIAGO, RAYMOND D.
SATTERWHITE, RUSTY T.
SAXTON, DENVER J.
SAYRE, KRISTY D.
SCALES, JOSEPHINE P.
SCANLON, MICHAEL A.
SCARBERRY, KYLE W.
SCHACH, CHESTER A.
SCHLUETER, MARK D.
SCHNEIDER, ROBERT E.
SCHOEPFLIN, DALE A.
SCHOEPPACH, STEVEN L.

SCHOOLCRAFT, THOMAS J.
SCHRACK, JAMES E.
SCHUERMANN, DERICK S.
SCHULER, RICHIE V.
SCHULTZ, TROY L.
SCHWARZ, JOHN R.
SCHWERDTFEGER, JESSE B.
SCOTT, BEN M.
SCOTT, BUSTER JR.
SCOTT, SUMMER S.
SCOTT, WILLIAM M.
SCRIBNER, JUSTIN D.
SCRIVNER, TIMOTHY L.
SCROGGINS, TERI E.
SCULLAWL, SHANE T.
SCULLY, HENRY P.
SEABOLT, RICHARD E.
SEALS, ROCKY L.
SEAY, AMBER D.
SEBOURN, JOE A.
SEBREE, ANDREW T.
SECREST, JOHN P.
SECREST, WILLIAM E.
SECREST, WILLIAM T.
SEIBERT, JAMES M.
SEIGLER, JARED A.
SEITZ, CHARLES R.
SELLERS, JESSIE W.
SELMAN, EDWARD S.
SEMLER, MICHAEL E.
SEVEDGE, NICHOLAS A.
SEVIGNY, ROLAND G.
SEYMOUR, DONALD T.
SHACKELFORD, MICHAEL P.
SHAHAN, LESLEY R.
SHARP, CHRISTOPHER L.
SHARP, JAKE W.
SHARP, JESSICA L.
SHARP, JUSTIN N.
SHARPE, STANFORD A.
SHATTUCK, DARREN D.
SHAUER, STEVEN M.

SHAW, DANIEL R.
SHAW, GILBERT R.
SHAWNEE, MARKUS W.
SHEA, FRANK W.
SHEAHAN, DENNIS R.
SHEARER, LOGAN R.
SHEARRER, ROBERT D.
SHED, JAMASON D.
SHELBY, DAVID H.
SHELITE, MICHAEL J.
SHELTON, JONATHAN E.
SHEPARD, PAUL E.
SHEPPARD, DAVID M.
SHEPPARD, JUDAH G.
SHERMAN, CATHERINE L.
SHERRILL, JOHN W.
SHIELDS, EUGEAN D.
SHOOK, CHRISTOPHER L.
SHORT, DEREK C.
SHORT, JUSTIN W.
SIBBLE, MONTANA W.
SILK, JAMES D.
SIMINGTON, ROBERT J.
SIMMONS, COREY D.
SIMMONS, ERIC M.
SIMMONS, HEATH M.
SIMMONS, LEVI G.
SIMMONS, SHAYNE M.
SIMONS, CHRISTOPHER C.
SIMPSON, DAVID B.
SIMPSON, TWYLA I.
SIMS, GEORGE E.
SIMS, KENNETH E.
SINCLAIR, LARRY L.
SKIPWORTH, SPENCER R.
SLATE, JAMES D.
SLATER, BRYON K.
SLAUGHTER, CHRISTOPHER
SLAUGHTER, KENNETH R.
SLEDGE, ANTHONY A.
SLEZICKEY, DAVID A.
SLIGER, JOSEPH R.

SLOAN, KRISTIN L.
SLOCTER, MICHAEL R.
SMART, TONY U.
SMIDDY, TRAVIS A.
SMITH, ADRIAN M.
SMITH, ANDREW R.
SMITH, CHRISTINE L.
SMITH, CHRISTOPHER L.
SMITH, CODY J.
SMITH, DALE A.
SMITH, DANIEL A.
SMITH, DARRYL L.
SMITH, DAVID R.
SMITH, DENNIS
SMITH, DEVIN L.
SMITH, DOYLE D.
SMITH, EARL D.
SMITH, EDWARD J.
SMITH, EVAN R.
SMITH, FRANK C.
SMITH, GREGORY A.
SMITH, HOPPER T.
SMITH, JAMES A.
SMITH, JAMES B.
SMITH, JAMES N.
SMITH, JAMES R.
SMITH, JASON R.
SMITH, JOHN T.
SMITH, JOSEPH K.
SMITH, JOSH L.
SMITH, JUSTIN C.
SMITH, KELLY D.
SMITH, KENNETH B.
SMITH, LARRY D.
SMITH, MICHAEL B.
SMITH, MICHAEL C.
SMITH, MIRANDA K.
SMITH, NICHOLAS L.
SMITH, RICHARD G.
SMITH, ROBERT D.
SMITH, SHAWN D.
SMITH, STEVEN L.

SMITH, JACK W.
SMITHERMAN, GREGORY D.
SMOTHERS, RODNEY E.
SMYTHE, TIMOTHY N.
SNIDER, JIM W.
SNOW, BOBBY G.
SNOW, CODY L.
SNOW, DANNY L.
SNYDER, AMANDA N.
SNYDER, BRIAN A.
SOCKEY, JEREMY W.
SOERGEL, IAN A.
SOLIS, CHRISTOPHER C.
SOLIS, RICARDO
SOLIS, RICHARD A.
SOLIZ, PEDRO JR.
SOPPET, GREGG F.
SOWARDS, ROBERT E.
SPANIER, LACY M.
SPANKE, ROBERT L.
SPASIC, MICHAEL N.
SPAULDING, CARL E.
SPELLER, CARLTON S.
SPENCER, GREGORY R.
SPENCER, JACKIE D.
SPENCER, RANDALL J.
SPITZER, BRUCE L.
SPIVA, GARY D.
SPIVEY, JEFFERY L.
SPRINGFIELD, SCOTT A.
STACEY, JAMES R.
STAGGS, SEAN M.
STALL, DOUGLAS E.
STANDLEE, SHEA D.
STANFILL, JOHN H.
STANFORD, STEVEN D.
STANLEY, ANTHONY B.
STANTON, JOHN R.
STAPLES, TASHEEN L.
STARR, CRAIG T.
STARR, WAYNE D.
STARRETT, STEVEN M.

STATON, JEANNE R.
STECKMAN, JUSTIN D.
STEED, CHRISTOPHER S.
STEELE, JOHN M.
STEELE, RICKY A.
STEELE, JOSEPH A.
STEFFEE, MATTHEW L.
STEGALL, GARRETT R.
STEGALL, STUARD J.
STEINMEYER, KELLY L.
STELLING, CODY L.
STEPHENS, CHARLES D.
STEPHENS, JOHN T.
STEPHENS, TONYA R.
STEVENS, BRITTIN M.
STEVENS, CHRISTOPHER L.
STEVENS, KEITH D.
STEVENS, NATHAN A.
STEVENSON, JEFFREY R.
STEVENSON, JERROD B.
STEWART, DARIL K.
STEWART, DAVID W.
STEWART, DENNIS O.
STEWART, WILLIAM J.
STEWART, ROBERT A.
STICE, JEFFREY A.
STICE, LARRY J.
STIER, RUSSELL W.
STILES, VINCENT W.
STILWELL, SCOTT A.
STIMMEL, WILLIAM E.
STOCKERT, COREY J.
STODDARD, ROBERT L.
STOKELY, DARREL W.
STOKES, DUSTIN L.
STOLIBY, DOUGLAS W.
STONE, JAMES M.
STONE, JOHN L.
STONE, MICHAEL J.
STONE, WILLIAM E.
STOTTS, JOHN C.
STOVALL, KIP J.

STOVER, ERIC M.
STOVER, JOE A.
STOVER, RICHARD M.
STOVER, JOE A.
STOWE, GREGORY J.
STRATTON, BARNEY O.
STRICKLAND, STEVEN M.
STRICKLIN, ALEX J.
STRICKLIN, JASON D.
STRICKLIN, LOGAN P.
STRINGER, EDWARD L.
STROOK, JERRY D.
STROUD, THOMAS B.
STROUP, WALLACE J.
STRUNK, MATTHEW R.
STUBBS, GEORGE A.
STUBBS, ROBERT D.
STUCKEY, PAMELYN R.
STUMBLINGBEAR, CHRISTOP
STURDEVANTCLINTON, III
STURGEON, CHRISTOPHER
STURGEON, LEWIS E.
STUTZMAN, CHRISTOPHER
SULLIVAN, CHRISTOPHER
SULLIVAN, KENNETH L.
SULLIVAN, STEVEN R.
SUMMERLIN, CHASE G.
SUMMERLIN, KEVIN L.
SUMNER, SHAWN M.
SUNDAY, ROBIN L.
SURBER, CHARLES R.
SUSMILCH, MICHAEL R.
SWAILS, DAVID S.
SWANN, PHILLIP T.
SWANSON, BRANDON S.
SWANSTON, ANDREW W.
SWARNES, BLAKE F.
SWART, NICHOLAS R.
SWARTZ, JOSHUA C.
SWEARENGIN, CODY L.
TACKETT, ANGELA R.
TALLANT, KENNETH T.

TALLEY, RAYMOND P.
TANQUARY, JODIE M.
TARRANT, MICHAEL S.
TASI, ARLINGTON N.
TATE, HERBERT D.
TATE, PAUL A.
TATE, MATTHEW J.
TATUM, JEWEL
TATUM, TONY S.
TATUM, WILLIAM R.
TAVIS, CHARLES C.
TAYLOR, BRANDON C.
TAYLOR, DAWN R.
TAYLOR, DOMINIC R.
TAYLOR, HARVETTA R.
TAYLOR, JASON W.
TAYLOR, JOHNNY D.
TAYLOR, MICHAEL D.
TAYLOR, MICHAEL E.
TAYLOR, MICHAEL E.
TAYLOR, RICHARD J.
TAYLOR, WENDY L.
TECHBUCKNER, BARBARA E.
TEEL, TERRANCE C.
TEETER, HEIDI M.
TEKAMP, EDWARD P.
TEMPEL, JOSHUA J.
TEMPLETON, SPENCER W.
TENNEFOS, CHARLES C.
TENNYSON, ANTHONY Q.
TERREL, RICHARD S.
THEISS, JOSHUA A.
THIEME, RANDY A.
THOMAS, CHRISTOPHER A.
THOMAS, JIMMY J.
THOMAS, MARGARET V.
THOMAS, RICHARD D.
THOMAS, WILLIAM C.
THOMAS, MITCHELL E.
THOMASON, JOHN T.
THOMPSON, ALAN R.
THOMPSON, CRAIG D.

THOMPSON, DAVID L.
THOMPSON, DOUGLAS J.
THOMPSON, HANNAH R.
THOMPSON, JOHN P.
THOMPSON, MICHAEL C.
THOMPSON, RAYMOND L.
THOMPSON, ROBERT E.
THOMPSON, SCOTT A.
THOMPSON, CLAYTON L.
THORNTON, ADAM D.
TIDABACK, KRISTEN D.
TIFFIE, CALVIN C.
TIGER, ANTHONY J.
TIGER, DANNY J.
TILLERY, MICHAEL K.
TILLMAN, DAVID L.
TINKHAM, CYNTHIA K.
TIPPETT, BRIAN R.
TIPSWORD, JOHN E.
TIPTON, MATTHEW P.
TITSWORTH, GARY R.
TITSWORTH, RONNIE D.
TITSWORTH, CHARLES K.
TOBEN, TONIA R.
TODD, MARK A.
TOLLISON, KENNETH S.
TOLSON, JERRY L.
TOMS, JOHN M.
TORBETT, ROBERT L.
TORRES, ANGEL E.
TORRES, RAUL
TOUMBS, MICHAEL A.
TOWLES, JOEL G.
TOWN, WILIAM D.
TOWNSEND, EDWARD R.
TRAMMELL, GEORGE R.
TRAMMELL, JOSHUA C.
TRAMMELL, TERRY G.
TREAGESSER, RYAN H.
TREANOR, MICHAEL B.
TRIM, VON E.
TRIMBLE, DEMITRI

TRIMBLE, RAYMOND C.
TROLLINGER, LARI D.
TROTTS, JARED H.
TROUT, BRIAN M.
TROUTMAN, BARRETT G.
TROYER, GREGG M.
TRYON, FRANCINE E.
TSOTIGH, PATRICK A.
TUCK, ERIC C.
TUCKER, KENNETH W.
TUCKER, LATOYA D.
TUCKER, PHILLIP B.
TUCKER, VERLYN E.
TUCKER, JASON E.
TUCKER, WILLIAM E.
TULLIS, MATHEW D.
TUNSTALL, RAILYN
TURBEVILLE, MATTHEW D.
TURLEY, MICHAEL C.
TURLINGTON, RICHARD E.
TURNER, CHRISTINE M.
TURNER, DARRON R.
TURNER, ROBERT L.
TURNEY, ANDREA E.
TUTTLE, JOHN M.
TYLER, DANIEL W.
TYLER, JEFFREY J.
TYLER, STEPHEN P.
TYLER, FOGLE D.
TYNER, NEAL W.
ULLRICH, JEREMY L.
ULRICH, TRAVIS L.
UMPHREY, WILLIAM J.
UNDERHILL, KELLY C.
UNDERNEHR, BRENT R.
UNDERWOOD, ANTHONY G.
UNDERWOOD, STEVEN R.
UPCHURCH, LEROY D.
UPDIKE, KENNETH L.
URBAN, HAROLD E.
URBAN, JACK W.
URRUTIA, GINA Y.

VADDER, SAMUEL H.	WAKEFIELD, JOEL D.	WATKINS, BRYAN S.	WHITE, LINDY I.	WILLIAMS, SPRINT D.
VAIL, BRANDON W.	WALCUTT, BENJAMIN E.	WATKINS, RICHARD B.	WHITE, ROBERT W.	WILLIAMS, KEVIN B.
VANAUSDALL, JOE D.	WALDRON, MICAH J.	WATKINS, WILLIAM F.	WHITE, WALTER T.	WILLIAMS, TRIPPER B.
VANCE, CASEY N.	WALKER, ALINE G.	WATSON, CHAVETTE D.	WHITE, GREGORY M.	WILLIAMS, WARREN P.
VANDERBURG, DANIEL B.	WALKER, BART L.	WATSON, JONATHAN R.	WHITE, JOEY K.	WILLIAMSON, JONATHAN C.
VANDERMEY, FRANCIS J.	WALKER, BILLY W.	WATSON, MATTHEW J.	WHITED, RICHARD C.	WILLIAMSON, CHERYL D.
VANESSENDELFT, LEROY D.	WALKER, JERRY W.	WATSON, CHRISTOPHER J.	WHITLOW, TIRELL F.	WILLIS, DARRICK A.
VANLANDINGHAM, BENTLEY	WALKER, JONI G.	WATTS, THOMAS C.	WHITMORE, JERRY L.	WILLOUGHBY, ERIC L.
VANLEER, CHARLES N.	WALKER, KEITH A.	WAY, JAMES L.	WHITSON, BILLY J.	WILLYARD, ISAAC A.
VANONI, ERICKA L.	WALKER, KENNETH P.	WAYLAND, GARY M.	WHITTINGTON, JAVAR R.	WILSON, AMANDA L.
VANONI, MICHAEL C.	WALKER, KURTIS W.	WAYLAND, MARK E.	WHITTINGTON, ROBERT W.	WILSON, ANDREW J.
VANWAGNER, DENNIS W.	WALKER, TIMOTHY T.	WEATHERBY, CYGEN R.	WHITTLE, DANIEL J.	WILSON, ANGELA K.
VARNER, BARTON R.	WALKER, VIRGIL D.	WEAVER, JEREMY D.	WHYATT, JOSEPH D.	WILSON, BRADLEY E.
VASQUEZ, FRANCISCO T.	WALLACE, EVAN R.	WEAVER, JOSHUA I.	WICK, BRIAN L.	WILSON, CARRIE I.
VAUGHAN, BENNIE R.	WALLACE, JOHN S.	WEBB, DAVID E.	WICKLIFFE, GUY P.	WILSON, DARIN L.
VAUGHAN, JACK P.	WALLACE, KALEB T.	WEBB, MICHAEL J.	WICKS, BILLY G.	WILSON, DAVID E.
VEGA, JOSE SR.	WALLACE, KEVIN E.	WEBBER, DANIEL G.	WICKSON, RAYMOND J.	WILSON, DAVID J.
VEIT, LARRY L.	WALLACE, NEAL P.	WEBER, MICHAEL L.	WIEDERKEHR, JOSHUA D.	WILSON, JONATHAN D.
VELASCO, MICHAEL R.	WALLACE, JAMES D.	WEEKS, BILLY J.	WILBURN, CHESTER M.	WILSON, JONATHAN K.
VELASQUEZ, ISSAC B.	WALLIS, BRIAN A.	WEEKS, DARRON P.	WILCOX, VAUGHN L.	WILSON, LEMARCUS J.
VELEZARMAN, ALEXIS L.	WALLS, DAVID M.	WEGER, KENDALL B.	WILDENHEIM, MICHAEL A.	WILSON, LEON E.
VELEZGONZALEZ, EFREN J.	WALLS, TED G.	WEIS, KARA S.	WILES, CHRISTOPHER J.	WILSON, MICHAEL G.
VENABLE, CRISTI L.	WALTER, ROBERT H.	WEISS, BENJAMIN J.	WILEY, DREW S.	WILSON, ROBERT D.
VERA, DAVID R.	WANGER, DANNY L.	WELLS, CHRISTOPHER W.	WILEY, STEVEN T.	WILSON, TREVOR R.
VERHINES, GARETT D.	WARD, CHAD T.	WELLS, JUSTIN B.	WILHAM, LOUIS W.	WILSON, WAYNE E.
VERMILLION, RICHARD D.	WARD, CLINTON T.	WELLS, RICKY A.	WILHITE, KEVIN L.	WILSON, WILLIAM D.
VERMILLION, LEONARD E.	WARD, DARVIN R.	WERNKE, MATTHEW J.	WILKENS, TIMOTHY E.	WILSON, CHRIS R.
VERNNON, ERIN R.	WARD, JOEL P.	WERNKE, PETER J.	WILKERSON, JODY J.	WILSON, CHRISTOPHER S.
VERNNON, MICHAEL A.	WARD, MICHAEL D.	WEST, ECHOTA L.	WILKERSON, JAMES W.	WILSON, CODY W.
VERON, SCOTT W.	WARE, BRIAN M.	WEST, NICOLE M.	WILKINSON, JASON L.	WILSON, ERIC L.
VICK, ROBERT M.	WARE, THEODORE M.	WEST, WILLIAM A.	WILLIAMS, BRUCE J.	WILSON, LAMAR H.
VINCENT, RODNEY J.	WARNER, DUSTIN E.	WHEELER, DAVID M.	WILLIAMS, BRYAN D.	WINCHESTER, JOSEPH W.
VIRGIN, STEPHEN C.	WARNER, JAMES C.	WHEELER, JAMIE K.	WILLIAMS, CAROLINE B.	WINDBERRY, JEROD W.
WADDELL, KEVIN M.	WARNER, BRIAN C.	WHEELER, LARRY J.	WILLIAMS, CHASE A.	WINGFIELD, CHAD R.
WADDELL, ZACKERY J.	WARNKE, AARON J.	WHEELER, MARCUS C.	WILLIAMS, DAVID K.	WINGO, KORY N.
WADE, BRIAN T.	WARREN, MICHAEL R.	WHEELER, AMETHYST M.	WILLIAMS, DAVID M.	WINKLE, KRISTI L.
WADE, ERIC M.	WARREN, CHRISTOPHER R.	WHELPLEY, JARED A.	WILLIAMS, DEREK P.	WINN, JEFFREY P.
WAGGONER, DANIELLE W.	WASHA, JASPER K.	WHETSTONE, GREGORY D.	WILLIAMS, JOHN F.	WINN, NORMAN L.
WAGGONER, GLEN M.	WASHINGTON, CHARLOTTE	WHISENHUNT, JERRY B.	WILLIAMS, LARRY D.	WINNINGHAM, JOSHUA T.
WAGNER, JERALD D.	WASSON, SAMUEL D.	WHITE, BONNIE L.	WILLIAMS, LOWELL J.	WINSTON, MARVIN E.
WAGONER, CHARLES R.	WATERS, DARYL L.	WHITE, CHRISTOPHER D.	WILLIAMS, MISTY D.	WINTERS, JOANN M.
WAHKAHQUAH, KARLI J.	WATERS, JASON R.	WHITE, JAMES A.	WILLIAMS, ROBERT B.	WIRGES, DANIEL V.

WISEMAN, JAMES W.
WISHON, DAVID R.
WOFFORD, CHAD J.
WOLF, ERIK A.
WOLF, TERRY W.
WOLFE, THOMAS E.
WOLFE, JOSHUA B.
WOMACK, BRANDON K.
WOMACK, DANIEL L.
WOMACK, TERRY W.
WOOD, CASEY L.
WOOD, JOSHUA C.
WOOD, MICHEAL D.
WOOD, MICHAEL L.
WOODALL, MARSDEN B.
WOODALL, ROCKY V.
WOODARD, CARLOS T.
WOODBERRY, LONNIE H.
WOODMAN, RANDY F.
WOODS, CHRISTOPHER L.
WOODS, DUSTIN L.
WOODS, MICHAEL L.
WOODY, FARGO A.
WOOLLEY, SHAWN M.
WOOLVER, JEREMY J.
WOOLVERTON, THOMAS Z.
WORLEY, RICHARD S.
WORLEY, RICHARD K.
WRIGHT, CRAIG J.
WRIGHT, DEMETRIUS A.
WRIGHT, ERIC W.
WRIGHT, HARRISON L.
WRIGHT, JOSEPH D.
WRIGHT, NICHOLAS A.
WRIGHT, ADAM L.
WUNDER, LANCE A.
WYATT, COLBY B.
WYATT, LARRY D.
WYLDER, TERRY L.
WYNNE, JIMMY J.
YACKESCHI, GLENDAL B.
YANDELL, BOBBY L.

YARBROUGH, ELISHA M.
YATES, CHRISTOPHER M.
YATES, CLINT D.
YATES, CRAIG A.
YATES, ROBERT S.
YBARRA, PHILLIP M.
YEAHQUO, TIMOTHY SR.
YOCHAM, DAVID E.
YOCHUM, STEPHEN M.
YODER, BRADLEY L.
YORK, BRYAN J.
YOST, WESLEY A.
YOUNG, AUSTIN T.
YOUNG, BRYAN J.
YOUNG, DAVID E.
YOUNG, DON A.
YOUNG, ERIC S.
YOUNG, JAMES T.
YOUNG, KELLY L.
YOUNG, MARKUS D.
YOUNG, MATTHEW A.
YOUNG, JOHN W.
ZARELLA, ANDREW D.
ZERGER, JONATHAN D.
ZICKEFOOSE, JESSE W.
ZIMMERMAN, DAVID L.
ZIMMERMAN, SKYLAR R.
ZINK, GLENN J.
ZIRK, LEROY C.

MEMBERS OF THE OKLAHOMA AIR NATIONAL GUARD

ABSHERE, PHIL
ADAMS, BRENT
ADAMS, WAYNE
AHERN, ROBERT J.
ALGER, ROBERT
ANGLE, DUSTIN
ASHFORD, BRADLEY J.
ASSAF, SARAH
ATCHLEY, CHRIS
BAIRD, ROBERT
BAKER, GLEN
BANSE, JOANN
BARNES, JASON
BATES, CLYDE
BATES, TRACEE
BEARDSLEY, DAVID P.
BENTLEY, CHARLES R.
BENTON, JOHNATHAN
BINA, CHERRY
BJAALAND, TARAH
BLEAKLEY, KRISTINE
BLICKENSDERFER, JOHN
BLOOMER, JAMES
BONTRAGER, SARA
BRADLEY, MARC
BRAGGS, WILLIE

BRANUM, GREG
BRINEGAR, LINDEL K.
BROWN, TIMOTHY
BROWN, TRAVIS
BROWNING, PETER J.
BRUCE, TREY
BUCHANAN, DEBBIE
BUCHANAN, RICK
BULLARD, DEIDRA
BURDETTE, GRIFFITH
BURKE, JAMES
BURRIS, BLAINE
BUSHEE, TONY M.
BUTLER, JACQUELINE
BUTTERS, BREWSTER
CALDWELL, PAUL J.
CALLUETTE, ERIC
CALVERY, ADAM
CAMERON, RANDY L.
CARETER, DONALD H.
CARMICHAEL, KENNETH
CARSON, BRUCE
CARTER, AMY
CASTLEMAN, JASON
CELESKI, COLLEEN
CHADDON, TROY M.

CHERNEY, CHRISTOPHER
CHRISTIAN, JUSTIN
CIARLO, REMO
CIKER, LLOYD D.
CLINE, ADAM
CLUFF, SPENCER
COBBLE, KELLY
CODY, JIMMY
COLLINS, SCOTT G.
CONELL, JOSEPH
CONNEL, MATT W.
CONNEL, TINA
COPE, SHARRI
COPELAND, MARK
CORTEZ, JIMMY
CORTEZ, LEROY
CORTNER, JOSH
COULTER, SCHERRYL
COWELL, SCOTT
COX, JESS W.
CRAIN, BRIAN
CROW, ROGER
CROZIER, BRENT
CUTTER, THOMAS L.
DALLAROSA, JOHN
DARLING, DONALD

DAUGHERTY, WILLIAM
DAVIS, KEITH
DEEDS-BUFORD, JACQUELINE
DELLA VECCHIO, RUDOLPH
DENNING, CHRIS
DERRICK, TAMARA
DODGE, MATTHEW
DOLL, SEAN R.
DORMAN, RICHARD R. II
DOZIER, ROY
DUCKWALL, NICOLE
DUDZINSKI, MICHAEL F.
DUFRIEND, PATRICK
DUNHAM, ROBERT E.
EASTER, NEELY
EBBS, JEFFREY
EGERT, GEOFFERY
ELLIS, JACOB M.
FANNING, MARLENE
FARRELL, MIKE
FEES, LYNN
FISHER, LLOYD
FLETES, CELESTE
FOOTE, EDWARD
FORD, CRYSTAL
FOSTER, ROCHELLE

FRANCO, MELISSA
FROST, TODD M.
GALLEMORE, JACK
GARCIA, JOSE
GARNER, RODNEY
GARRETSON, DOUGLAS
GONZALES, MARGARET
GORDON, BILLY
GORDON, PETER
GREEN, MICHAEL A.
GRIGSBY, STEVEN
GRIMES, KELVIN
GROUND, KENNETH
GUEST, ROBERT
HADAWAY, WILLIAM
HALEY, THOMAS E. III
HAMILTON, JUSTIN
HAMMOND, PAUL
HARDERSON, AMANDA
HARRIS, ROY
HARRISON, MICHAEL S.
HAWKINS, LLOYD
HAYNES, MIKE
HEGINBOTHAM, ROYDEN
HEISER, DANIEL
HENDRICKSON, SCOTT

HEPNER, MIKE
HILDEBRANDT, DERRICK
HILL, MARK
HINSPERGER, ADAM D.
HOGAN, TRACEY
HOLMAN, DUSTIN C.
HOLT, DONALD
HOWARD, CHRISTOPHER P.
HOWARD, TERRY
ILES, JOSHUA
IRWIN, SCOTT R.
IVINS, DOUG
JASASARA, SARA
JOHNSON, DASHA
JOHNSON, DOUGLAS
JOHNSON, LEROY
JOHNSON, MICHAEL H.
JOHNSON, TERRELL
JOHNSTON, JEFFREY
JONES, JEFFREY L.
KEEL, JOHN
KEELY, DAVID
KENT, TIFANI
KERNS, JOHN
KILGORE, VINCE
KILMER, WILLIAM J.
KIM, JUN
KINNE, JESSICA
KIRKPATRICK, BEN
KOEHLER, ROGER
LACKMAN, ANTHONY
LAIN, GARY J.
LANE, KYLE
LARRISON, LYNN E.
LEATHERS, JOHN E.
LEEHAN, BRUCE W.
LEVERING, STEVEN D.
MALOY, KIM
MARKHAM, JOSHUA
MARTIN, CHRISTOPHER
MARTIN, KATY
MASDEN, MIKE

MASTON, PAUL
MAYBERRY, JEFF J.
MAYS, DAVID E.
MAYS, DAVID E.
MAYS, JAMES
MCCAINE, WILLIAM III
MCCALL, TRACY
MCCORMACK, DAVID A.
MCCORMACK, JOHN P.
MCCORMACK, MICHAEL
MCCUMBER, TIMOTHY
MCDONALD, MITCHELL J.
MCGILL, BRITTON
MCGINNITY, THOMAS
MCGUIRK, WESTON
MCMAHON, STACEY
MCMASTERS, DAVID
MCMURRY, KATHY
MEYN, ERIC D.
MILLER, DAVID
MILLER, RAMONA
MILLER, SCOTT L.
MILLS, KERRY
MISER, TERRY
MONTGOMERY, SCOTT
MOORE, ROY
MORENO, RICHARD
MORTON, DAVID
MOULTON, MARCUS
MUCKEY, MARK A.
MUNDAY, MARTHA
MYERS, GERALD
NILKUMHANG, ARLENE
NOWLIN, JOE
O'HARA, SEAN
ODPARLIK, MICHAEL A.
ODQUIST, JOSHUA M.
OWEN, BRET
OWENS, PATRICK
PAYNE, CORY
PELLEY, ROBERT
PHILLIPS, JOHN K.

PINKSTON, LADONNA
PORTER, RICHARD
POSTLEWAITE, JIM
PRYKRYL, NANCY
RAY, CASEY D.
REED, KEITH
REEVES, GERALD
RHODES, RITA
RICHARDSON, DUSTIN
RIGGLE, NATALIA
RIPPY, MAUREEN
RITZ, STEPHANIE
ROBERTSON, JOHN
ROBINSON, WILLIAM J.
ROGALSKI, CHRISTOPHER
ROGERS, AMANDA
ROGERS, JEREMY
ROGERS, LANCE
ROLLERSON, CATHERINE
ROSEBROOK, STEPHEN
ROZNECK, JASON P.
ROZNECK, MALLETTE
RYAN, THOMAS
SALGADO, ERIC O.
SANDERS, JAMES C.
SANDERSON, DENNIS
SCHADEL, GREG
SCHOTTER, JANE
SCOTT, EDDIE
SCOTT, JON
SELVEY, TYLER
SHAFER, DAVID R.
SHAFER, ROBERT
SHAW, TRACY
SHIPMAN, ANDY
SHIRLEY, MICHAEL A.
SIMPSON, ED
SLATER, DAN
SLATER, DAN J. JR.
SMALLEY, GEORGE
SMITH, DANIEL K.
SMITHSON, CODY

SMITHSON, EVERETT LLOYD
SNIDER, MICHAEL J.
SOLLERS, REX
SPENCER, TAMMY
SPENCER, TRACY
SPYCHALSKI, JOSEPH
STANLEY, DREW
STOW, CATE
SUDDATH, GERALD E.
SURBER, JAMES
SUTTON, ROBERT G.
SWANK, TODD
TALBERT, JUSTIN
TATE, DARCY
TAYLOR, ROBERT
TAYLOR, TY A.
TAYS, MICHAEL
TEEGARDEN, BETH
THOMAS, MICHAEL W.
THOMPSON, CAROLYN
THOMPSON, MICHAEL
TINSLEY, ELIZABETH
TIPPETT, CHRISTINA
TOWNSEND, SCOTT
TROTTER, RICHARD L.
TUCKER, KEVIN
TURNER, JOSEPH
UTSLER, DENNIS D.
VANMETER, BRETT A.
VAUGHAN, HENRY
VETTER, AARON
WALKER, CARLA
WALKER, JUSTIN W.
WALLACE, CHRISTOPHER
WALLER, JOHNNY W.
WARD, MICHAEL A.
WARDLAW, AARON S.
WARNER, PAUL
WATKINS, JARRIETT D.
WATSON, BERRY D.
WATTS, TIMOTHY
WEBB, BRENT

WEBB, FRANK
WEBB, MATTHEW R.
WESLEY, JOHN
WESTOVER, ALAN
WHALEY, THOMAS B.
WHITAKER, YVONNE
WHITE, ANDREW
WHITE, ANTHONY
WHITING, SUE
WHITMAN, ERIC B.
WILKINSON, JEFFREY M.
WILLBANKS, JAMES
WILLE, HENRY J.
WILLIS, JAMES
WINT, GRADY
WOODEN, DEVIN R.
WORKING, KENNETH R.
YAHNE, ANGELA
ZINN, NOAH

INDEX